101 Ways to Beat the Gas Pump

101 Ways to Beat the Gas Pump

✦

The First in a Series
Instructions for People Who Do Not Read Instructions

Andrew P. Noakes

iUniverse, Inc.
New York Lincoln Shanghai

101 Ways to Beat the Gas Pump
The First in a Series
Instructions for People Who Do Not Read Instructions

iUniverse books may be ordered through booksellers or by contacting:

iUniverse
2021 Pine Lake Road, Suite 100
Lincoln, NE 68512
www.iuniverse.com
1-800-Authors (1-800-288-4677)

Because of the dynamic nature of the Internet, any Web addresses or links contained in this book may have changed since publication and may no longer be valid.

ISBN: 978-0-595-44379-6 (pbk)
ISBN: 978-0-595-88708-8 (ebk)

Printed in the United States of America

The views expressed in this work are solely those of the author and do not necessarily reflect the views of the publisher, and the publisher hereby disclaims any responsibility for them.

Limit of liability and disclaimer of warranty: The author and publisher of this book would like to remind the readers that driving safely always comes first. Safe and efficient driving is of the utmost importance. Always abide by traffic laws and treat fellow motorists as you would like to be treated. The publisher and author of this book have given their best efforts in preparing this book. The publisher and author make no representations or warranties regarding the accuracy or completeness of the contents of this book and disclaim any implied warranties of merchantability. No warranties are extended beyond the descriptions contained in this paragraph. No warranty may be created or generated in any fashion by sales representatives or written sales materials. The accuracy and completeness of the information provided in this book are not guaranteed or warranted to produce any particular results. The ideas, procedures and suggestions made in this book are not intended as a substitute for your vehicle manufacturers' maintenance procedures or schedules. Additionally, the ideas, procedures, and suggestions presented in this book are in no way intended as a substitute from consulting with your mechanic in reference to repair and maintenance operations. The reader should also be aware that some repair and maintenance operations can bring you in contact with high voltages; hot, scalding, or harmful fluids; and dangerous moving parts. The advice, procedures, and strategies contained within this book may not be suitable for every individual. It is understood that this book is written with the sincere desire that the tips will improve fuel efficiency, save money at the gas pump, and improve the environment we live in. It is absolutely not this author's intent to encourage readers or drivers to take any risks while driving for the sake of saving fuel or any other reason. It is the reader's and driver's responsibility not to engage in any driving habit that could be deemed dangerous or against the law. It is also the reader's and driver's responsibility to drive within their experience, skill, or comfort level. Neither the publisher nor the author shall be responsible for any potential liability incurred by inaccuracy of or reader misinterpretation of statements. Neither the publisher nor the author shall be liable for any loss of profit or any other damage, including but not limited to special, incidental, consequential, or other damages.
No part of this publication may be reproduced in any fashion without the prior written consent of the copyright owner.

Contents

Acknowledgments

I sincerely want to acknowledge the people who helped bring this book to fruition:

First of all, my family. To my wife Janis for her patience and approval in supporting me and my ideas. To my children for the motivation that their/ our future will hold a much healthier and cleaner environment. To my mother for consistently advocating higher education.

Gwyn Erwin, for her help and encouragement in motivating me through periods of doubt. Her ideas, knowledge, and experience were invaluable in getting this book to press.

David Harrington, whose fun and whimsical illustrations helped breathe life into the concepts of this book.

Preface

✦

A Personal Initiative and a Call to Arms

There are volumes of information available today about saving money on gasoline; this information often discusses things you can do while driving your car or tips you can follow while at the pump. The truth of the matter is that most everyone is frustrated with the constantly increasing price of gasoline. We all want to dramatically lessen our financial burden and our dependency on oil. This book will show you how to reduce your fuel costs, no matter what you drive. If you are tired of high gas prices and want to reduce the amount of money you spend mile after mile, day after day, year after year, then this is the book for you. This book will pay for itself over and over.

Believe it or not, gas prices in the United States have been low for decades. We as a nation have enjoyed this luxury without realizing it. Gas prices around the world have almost always been higher than in the United States. According to Nationmaster.com and using the US liquid liter per gallon conversion of 3.785 liters per 1 US gallon, Uruguay has the highest premium gasoline prices at 1.95 dollars per liter or $7.38 per US gallon. The second and third highest prices are paid by the United Kingdom and Israel at $7.30 and $7.07 per US gallon respectively. The three lowest prices paid per US gallon in the world belong to Turkmenistan, Iraq and Iran at .11¢, $.19¢ and $.30¢ per US gallon respectively. I'm guessing that gasoline is less expensive than water in these three countries.

Nationmaster.com ranked 141 countries. Uruguay ranked #1, the UK #2 and Israel #3 as the highest prices paid per US gallon. Turkmenistan was ranked #141, Iraq was #140 and Iran was #139 as the lowest prices per US gallon. The US ranked #102 out of the 141 countries.

The following cartoon depicts how violated many of us throughout the world feel at the pump.

The time has come for us to take the initiative to reduce our expenditures and our dependency on oil. The good news is that we Americans have proven throughout our history that we are up for a challenge. Rising to the occasion is in our blood, our heritage, and our culture. It is my hope that this book generates a sense of urgency amongst us, and I hope it helps you save hundreds, if not thousands of dollars each year.

In addition to being what I hope is a money-saving book for you, I also hope that using less gasoline becomes a personal initiative and a call to arms, so to speak, to help save our environment.

Introduction

According to the Energy Information Administration's Basic Petroleum Statistics, total world petroleum consumption is approximately eighty-four million barrels, or more than 3.5 billion gallons per day (EIA). It makes me wonder why the world hasn't caved in yet. Just kidding. But you have to agree that these numbers are just staggering.

The United States consumes more than twenty million barrels or over eight hundred seventy three million gallons of oil each day. Of this, three hundred eighty four million seven hundred thousand of these gallons is used daily as finished motor gasoline. Yep, *each day*. Can you believe it?

Two hundred million motor vehicles are driven more than seven billion miles per day in the United States. That's right; I said *seven billion* miles. Let's expand this information a little further. In the United States alone, we are driving more than two hundred fifty billion miles per year. That's a lot of miles. That distance traveled translates to millions of additional dollars spent at the pump when gas prices increase just a few cents. Amazing, isn't it?

But wait, I'm not done …

Take the three hundred eighty four million seven hundred thousand gallons of gasoline used daily in the United States and multiply that by the cost of a gallon of gasoline. When I wrote this chapter, a gallon of regular unleaded gasoline cost $3.37 in my town. This means that approximately 1.3 billion dollars is being spent daily on gasoline in the United States. That's a lot of money.

But wait, I'm still not done …

Now, take the above approximate daily expenditure on gasoline in the U.S. and multiply it times four (because the United States consumes approximately 25 percent of the world's petroleum products) to get the amount of money spent each day for gasoline around the world. Using the $3.37 cost of gas in my town as a world average (which I think is very conservative) the world spends approximately 5.2 billion dollars a day on gasoline. Wow! I had no idea, and I would guess you had no idea how much money we spend on gasoline each day. I have to say it again, Wow!

The things I have learned in life and in business apply to this book. I have learned to stay on track and achieve many things by having goals, a purpose, and a mission. The *goals* of this book are to educate the reader about ways to be a more environmentally conscious driver by being aware of the way they drive. The *purpose* of this book is to help you, the reader, save money at the gas pump and to improve the health of our environment. The *mission* of the "Instructions for People Who Do Not Read Instructions" series is to help people live better, healthier lives without overcomplicating things.

I hope to have written a book that will appeal to your sensibilities as well as your pocketbook. I hope these writings will encourage you to make a conscious and ongoing effort to change the way you drive and to use far less gasoline as a result.

What would happen if we were able to decrease our oil and gas consumption by 10 percent, 20 percent, or even 30 percent? These are very real and easily achieved goals. I used four cars as test vehicles while gathering information to write this book. On average, I have been able to decrease my gasoline consumption by more than 30 percent.

This started me thinking, and I began to imagine the chain of events or the chain of possibilities. What if this type of change could occur for all the drivers in my family? What if this amount of change could be had for all the families in my neighborhood or in my town? What could potentially happen if the human race significantly reduced our consumption and dependency on gasoline by continuing to expand on this idea countywide, statewide, nationwide, or even worldwide? The effect could be profound. In the United States, we may not decrease the seven billion miles we drive each day, but we can significantly decrease the three hundred eighty four million seven hundred thousand gallons of gasoline we consume each day.

Another huge benefit would leave an equally profound and lasting impact; we could significantly reduce the pollution being released into our environment.

The potential of the above-described chain of events is extremely inspiring to me, and it is achievable. To some, the savings can and will become reality. To others, the savings are simply wishful thinking. And to others still, the ideas may sound too good to be true.

The reality is that if enough people take this book and their driving habits seriously, we can actually improve our world, our environment, and our lives while fattening our pocketbooks. Driving efficiently is such an easy thing to do; it really does not have to be a fantasy. Fatter wallets and a better environment could become our reality. If you really think about the ideas to come, if each of you really tries to change the way you drive, we all can improve our world and fatten our pocketbooks.

How to Use This Book

What do we really know about driving? We attended driver's education training, we memorized the rules of the road, and we picked up most of our driving habits by observing our parents, friends, and siblings. But how much instruction were we actually given about the proper way to use our cars? The information in this book will help you learn to drive your car more efficiently, help you save money on gasoline and teach you to drive in consideration of a healthier environment.

This book is designed in a way that allows you to take advantage of the tips in any order you see fit. You can read the pages from cover to cover; you can select a chapter that interests you the most; or you can skip around as you like.

All too often, books such as this one are eagerly read and quickly set aside. Some people will read this book and really understand it and use it consistently. Most people will understand its ideas but will not implement them as well, as often, or as consistently as they should. The problem is that information is only the beginning.

Most people, like I said, understand the ideas but don't follow through on implementing them. We are torn between understanding and doing. Action is the missing piece of the puzzle. I think we all want to save money and live in a healthier environment, but our mind-set gets in the way. We can overcome this mind-set by taking action.

There are hundreds of ideas in this book that will help you save money at the gas pump. I strongly suggest that you not try all of them at once. Doing so will prove to be overwhelming, and you will probably give up before you see any results. Instead, choose to implement a few of these ideas for one week, or for as long as it takes you to go through a tank of gas. Choose ideas that you consider to be the easiest or the most likely to work for your driving style. At the end of the trial period, see how well you did. I imagine you'll do quite well and that you'll be pleased with your efforts. I hope the positive results will motivate you to try more tactics and ultimately save more money.

A question I have been asked repeatedly is, "How can I save a lot of money at the pump without changing my driving style too much?"

Initially, I didn't have an answer. As I thought about the question and spent time researching this book, the answer eventually presented itself to me. The answer is that my mind-set began to evolve. The more I learned and the more success I had in saving money at the pump, the more I was motivated to continue how I was changing my driving style. As you can see, I was motivated enough to write a book about it.

I encourage and challenge you not to just read this book but to also apply what you learn to your daily driving habits. I want this book to help you be successful in saving money at the pump because I would love for you to have more money in your pocket.

I found all of the gas-saving tips in this book to be successful, and I discovered that no single tip was able to create a massive increase in the number of miles I was able to drive per gallon of gasoline. It was a cumulative effort.

I also found that all of the gas-saving tips started to work immediately upon implementation. I hope you will find this to be true as well. With a reasonable amount of effort, the average driver should, if they follow the instructions in this book, be able to decrease their gasoline consumption 15 percent to 25 percent.

You will be most successful if you view beating the gas pump as a fun thing to do. I found that challenging myself each week kept me interested in the task at hand. It also made driving fun again, despite traffic.

The icons described below are to be used as a quick reference guide. They will assist you in identifying the gas-saving tips that are listed throughout this book. These icons are designed to be a fun way to help you understand the meaning of each of the tips by creating a visual reminder. The tips with the most icons have the greatest savings potential.

This icon is used to illustrate gas savings you can obtain by accelerating gently and carefully. You can save a lot of money on gas, and you'll save your car a lot of unnecessary wear and tear.

This icon is used to remind you to stop a bad driving habit, one that is costing your pocketbook dearly, and replace it with a new, good driving habit.

This icon serves as a visual reminder of how expensive it can be to drive without consideration of the gas-saving tips in this book.

When a tip is accompanied by this icon, you will know that you are looking at one of the book's top-ten tips.

When a tip is accompanied by this icon, you will know that you are looking at one of the book's top-twenty tips.

This icon identifies tips that have great potential for saving you money, plus other benefits like less wear and tear on your car and the production of less pollutants.

This icon serves as a reminder for you to pay attention to what you are doing. It is meant to support you as you attempt to change the way you drive.

This icon is designed to help you change the way you do things. It will appear each time a common driving error is listed.

This icon reminds you to not drive aggressively, and not to drive too fast or with a "Lead Foot".

Remember, you are the driver; you are in control of what you drive and how you drive it. I am confident that you will soon see dramatic results. Good luck, and happy driving.

First Gear:
The Way You Drive

I almost called this chapter, "Your Lead Foot." All jokes aside, almost without question, the best way for you to save gas is by controlling your right foot. Nothing you do mechanically to change your car will have as much of a positive effect on your gas mileage as changing the way you drive. It is reported on www.Edmunds.com that drivers can save up to 37 percent of gasoline consumption by changing their driving habits (Reed and Hudson May 2006).

I discovered that the more tips I used, the more I saved. I was successful because I wanted to be successful. I will admit that I used to be a bit of a lead foot. My driving habits were very poor when it came to gas-savings techniques. I proved the Edmunds report to be true. I saved the most money and increased my fuel efficiency the greatest by simply changing my driving hab-its.

My research was conducted on the road, not in a lab. I was able to improve my average fuel efficiency by more than 30 percent, and I did so mostly by altering my driving style. I was also able to reproduce my results across four very different vehicles. I believe, and I hope, that great gas savings are waiting for you as well.

Let's start from the beginning. Let's start before you even get into your car to start it.

1. You *can* leave home without it (your car that is).

Now, here's a radical idea. Come to think of it, this may not actually be a *driving tip*, but, if at all possible, don't use your car. You will not con-sume any gas and you will not pollute the environment if you walk or ride a bike. As a great side effect, you'll improve your physical health. Be creative, have fun, save gas, save money, and get healthy.

2. Think about and plan your trip before you even get into your car.

This idea may sound so obvious that it is absurd to even include it in this book. However, many of us continue to use our cars to travel short dis-tances and run brief errands. Some of us even get into our cars and drive just to get gas.

You should ask yourself, "Is this trip really necessary? Can it be com-bined with another errand? Can I accomplish this task on my way to work or on my way home from work? Can I get this errand done by any other means?"

Come to think of it, how about entertaining the idea of using a different set of wheels. You could use roller skates, a scooter, or maybe a skateboard.

Bonus tip: Try to reduce the frequency of individual trips you make to buy one item at your local shopping mall or convenience store. If you shop daily for groceries or other items, you can decrease the frequency of these trips by combining trips or by doing your shopping weekly, by phone, or online. When you take your dog for a walk, tackle an errand at the same time. Can you use the phone, telecommute or use your computer to eliminate an errand?

Bonus tip: If you've ordered a pizza, a new refrigerator, or anything that can be delivered, determine if it is cost effective to have the item brought to you.

Making an effort to eliminate or consolidate your trips will save you money at the pump, wear and tear on your car, and probably time in your day.

3. Make all your driving preparations before you start your engine.

All too often, we get into our car, start it, and then take time to get comfortable. We clean off the windows, fix our hair, put on makeup, shave, put on our seatbelt, secure our cup of coffee, and adjust our seat and mirrors. This means your car is idling, polluting, and burning up expensive fuel while you are getting nowhere. This actually has a negative effect on your miles per gallon because fuel is being consumed and you are stationary. Do you realize that you are getting *negative* miles per gallon?

4. Avoid idling too long.

According to an article entitled "Idling: Myths Versus Reality," from the Office of Energy Efficiency in Canada, if you're going to be stopped for ten seconds or more, except in traffic, you should turn your engine off ("Idling: Myths Versus Reality").

The article goes on to say, "Contrary to popular belief, idling isn't an effective way to warm up your vehicle, even in cold weather. The best way to warm it up is to drive it. In fact, with today's engines, you need no more than 30 seconds of idling on winter days before you start to drive. The notion that idling is good for your vehicle is passé—in fact, it hasn't been the right thing to do since the advent of computer controlled engines. The truth is that excessive idling can damage the engine" ("Idling: Myths Versus Reality").

The article explains, "An idling engine isn't operating at its peak temperature, which means that fuel doesn't undergo complete combustion.

This leaves fuel residues that can condense on cylinder walls, where they can contaminate oil and damage parts of the engine. For example, fuel residues are often deposited on spark plugs. As you spend more time idling, the average temperature of the spark plug drops. This makes the plug get dirty more quickly, which can increase fuel consumption by 4% to 5 %. Excessive idling also lets water condense in the vehicle's exhaust. This can lead to corrosion and reduce the life of the exhaust system. Besides, what's often forgotten is that idling warms only the engine—not the wheel bearings, steering, suspension, transmission, and tires. These parts also need to be warmed up and the only way to do that is to drive the vehicle" ("Idling: Myths Versus Reality").

5. Don't rev the engine.

This is a big waste of gas.

6. Monitor your trip computer, fuel efficiency gauge, or miles per gallon economy meter.

A fuel efficiency gauge or miles per gallon economy meter, is a great feature to have on a car. If you have one, turn it on and let it monitor your driving habits. These types of gauges or trip computers are located on your dashboard, and they give you continuous feedback about how you are driving.

These meters are basically onboard computers that calculate your present miles per gallon, your average speed, and the number of miles you can travel based on how much gasoline is left in your tank and your current driving habits.

7. Monitor your tachometer.

You may think, "My tach-what-o-meter? I didn't know I had one." Your tachometer is a gauge on your dashboard that gives you constant feedback about how fast your engine is running. It is often located next to the speedometer. If your car does not have a fuel efficiency gauge or a miles per gallon meter, your tachometer is the next best thing to measure fuel efficiency.

The tachometer registers your engine's revolutions per minute, abbreviated rpm, in terms of thousands of revolutions per minute. As a general rule of thumb, the lower your revolutions per minute, the less fuel you are using, and the better fuel efficiency you are getting.

8. Lighten up, lead foot.

Avoiding heavy-footed or hard acceleration is a big gas saver. The amount of gas used to get a car rolling is great, and each time you come to a stop you have to get the car rolling again. That means the engine has to overcome the car's total weight, some two thousand to six thousand pounds (that's 1 to 3 tons). Some cars are even heavier. Let's put this into perspective. Have you ever had the misfortune to have had to push your car? If you have, you quickly become aware of its weight. If you haven't had the opportunity to push your car, imagine needing to push a medium-sized elephant on wheels.

Now, imagine having to do this hundreds of times each day. Your engine has to move one to three tons of glass, plastic, rubber, and steel each time you accelerate from a stopped position.

Accelerating *gently* from a dead stop and giving the car some time to get up to speed will significantly increase your miles per gallon. Smooth acceleration is a key element in saving money on gas.

Speeding, rapid acceleration, and hard braking will lower your gas mileage significantly. That quick start off the line costs you hundreds of dollars each year because aggressive driving and hard acceleration consume a great deal of gas. You probably do not need to press the accelerator more than 10 percent to 15 percent of its foot travel to get the car going. More than this is wasteful. Foot travel is the overall distance your gas pedal can travel from when you first touch it to when you have it pressed completely on the floor.

Here is a great visual (don't really do it or you'll have a big mess in your car) to help remind you not to stomp the gas pedal every time you accelerate. Pretend (and I do mean pretend) that there is an uncooked egg between the sole of your right foot and the gas pedal in your car like the icon shown above. The game is to gently accelerate without crushing the egg. The goal is for you to develop the sensitivity needed to best manipulate your gas pedal.

By learning to feather the gas pedal (not crushing the egg) you will get a feel for your car's acceleration as you discover its sweet spot (the cars optimal fuel efficient driving speed) while cruising down the highway. According to the California Energy Commission Consumer Energy Center, "While each vehicle reaches its optimal fuel economy at a different speed (or range of speeds), gas mileage usually decreases rapidly at speeds above 55 miles per hour. Just slowing down from 65 mph to 55mph can increase your miles per gallon by as much as 15 percent" (Speeding and Your Vehicles Mileage). This article continues, "According to the U.S. Department of Energy (DOE), as a rule of thumb, you can assume that each 5 mph you drive over 60 mph is like paying an additional $0.21 per gallon for gas (at $3.00 per gallon)."

9. Avoid hard braking.

Always be safe, but try to avoid hard braking when possible. Braking gradually will give you better control of your car, and you may not need to slow the car down as much or come to a complete stop as often. That constant on-again off-again activity between acceleration and braking consumes gas, and it costs you unnecessary wear and tear on your engine and brakes. Overcoming inertia (getting the car moving from a dead stop) is a big waste of gas, so try to keep your car in motion as much and as safely as possible.

In tip number eight, I discussed learning to best control your gas pedal by pretending to place an uncooked egg underfoot. I suggest you get to know the feel of your brakes just as well by pretending there is an egg between your foot and the brake pedal. Learning the feel of your brakes under various driving and stopping conditions is equally important as learning the feel of your gas pedal.

This is especially true if your car has an antilock braking system (ABS). When depressed hard and fast, a car with ABS will feel like your brake pedal is vibrating or pulsating underfoot. It can also feel like your brakes are skipping or slipping a little. This is a very different reaction than the one you will get in a car without ABS. Cars without ABS often lockup the wheels or feel like the brakes get stuck when depressed hard and fast. This is why getting to know the feel of your brakes is important.

Bonus tip: Here's a freebie. To some this tip may seem stupid, but I'll add it anyway. Make sure that your parking brake is fully released. I know, I know, it's obvious; but I must confess that I've failed to make this check before.

10. Take your shoes off.

In tips numbers eight and nine, I mentioned the need to get a feel for your gas and brake pedal. If you feel comfortable and safe doing this, take off your shoes so you can get a better feel for the gas pedal. (Remember to adjust your seating position to best control your car.) This tip will help you develop a far greater sensitivity to the amount of pressure you need to apply to the gas pedal, but please only do this if you feel safe.

"But I thought it was illegal to drive barefoot," you say? This is actually an urban myth. According to Jason R. Heimbaugh, the author of "Driving Barefoot in America," barefoot driving is legal (1994). You should of course verify the law for the state you are driving in. I would also suggest that you read Jason's article. It is available online at http:/ tafkac.org/legal/driving.barefoot/driving_barefoot.html

Bonus tip: Another thing to consider is the type of shoe you wear while driving. Race car drivers have special shoes so they can get the best feel of the accelerator, clutch, and brake. It only makes sense to consider the shoes you wear while driving. Heavy or awkward shoes will decrease your pedal sensitivity.

Bonus tip: Your attire (not just your shoes) will also play a role in your fuel efficiency because your clothes will guide your use of the air conditioner, windows, sunroof, and heater.

11. Travel in higher gears, or use your overdrive gear.

Traveling in a higher gear or using your overdrive gear will allow you to consume less fuel and save more money because your engine will be running at a lower rate of revolutions per minute. Running your motor fast in low gears pollutes more, consumes a lot of fuel, and puts a lot of needless wear and tear on the engine and transmission.

Most cars sold today come equipped with an automatic transmission. All the gears, including the overdrive gear, are almost always engaged automatically in an automatic transmission. An overdrive gear is an extra gear used when the car is traveling at higher rates of speed. It's like having a fourth gear in a three-speed car. The overdrive gear permits the car to maintain its speed while having fewer revolutions per minute. Having said this, some cars come equipped with a small button located near or on the stick shift that the driver can depress to select overdrive. Cars with a manual transmission do not have this feature because the driver is in control of what gear the transmission is in.

Bonus tip: Don't use your transmission to slow you down; this wastes gas. When you downshift, you throw the transmission into a lower gear and the car is revving at a lot higher rate. This decreases your miles per gallon. It is also very hard on your very expensive transmission.

12. Reduce your speed.

Lower speeds will save you a lot of money at the pump. The faster you go, the more fuel you use. This is because the faster you go, the more aerodynamic drag you create; this decreases fuel efficiency.

In other words, the faster you drive, the more wind or air you are bumping into. Here's a good visual (don't do this if you're the driver). Remember when you were a kid and you would hold your hand out the window pretending your hand was flying up and down in the wind like a plane? Well, try it again. When a flat hand is held out of the window of a moving car, aerodynamic drag is low. However, when you turn your hand upright, (now your hand looks like a sail) aerodynamic drag increases dramatically. Do you feel the difference? Do you feel the wind pushing your hand backward when it's a sail? That is aerodynamic drag.

I imagine that anyone who has ever been in a car with the windows open will know the different feelings of pressure depending upon how the hand is held against the oncoming wind. When your fingers point into the wind, your hand is able to easily slip through the oncoming air. When your hand is flat and turned into the wind, it becomes a small sail that catches the wind. Catching the wind in the sails is great for a boat, but lousy for a car.

Now, let's get back to cars. In order to overcome the weight and the very large surface area and/or drag created by the size and shape of your car, the engine must work hard. Size and weight really make a huge difference in your fuel consumption. An extreme example of aerodynamic and weight differences can be seen when one considers the differences between a sleek race car and a delivery truck or a big rig. This image makes it easy to visualize the differences.

There is a great demand for fuel to initially get a car rolling, as was discussed in tip number eight. Equally, there is a great continuous demand for fuel due to aerodynamic drag at higher speeds. Therefore, increasing speed decreases your miles per gallon. According to an article from www.fueleconomy.gov., "Aggressive driving (speeding, rapid accel-eration, and braking) wastes gas. It can lower your gas mileage by 33% at highway speeds and by 5% around town" (Driving More Efficiently).

I have one last comment on this topic. The faster you drive, the more you increase the chances of getting into an accident or getting a speeding ticket. Do yourself and everyone around you a favor and slow down.

13. Obey the speed limit.

Never exceed posted speed limits. First of all, the limits posted on our streets and highways are maximum speeds, not minimum speeds like many people seem to think. These limits are set for safety purposes. When followed, they also equal gas savings. The old speed limit of 55 mph was far more fuel efficient than the modern speed limit of 65 mph on most of our country's highways. According to an article from www.fueleconomy.gov., "Driving too fast beyond posted highway speed limits can increase your fuel consumption by 7% to 23%" (Driving More Efficiently).

14. Steady as she goes.

Frequent acceleration and slowing down wastes fuel. It is best to drive at a steady pace. Stop-and-go traffic consumes a lot of gas because every time you accelerate from a stop you use a lot of gas to overcome the weight of your car. By being gentle on the gas pedal you use less gasoline. By minimizing brake use and maintaining the momentum gained during acceleration you will use less fuel. Maintaining momentum is fuel efficient, braking is fuel inefficient. Each time you accelerate from a stop, you must overcome a lot of inertia. The less frequently you need to overcome inertia, the less fuel you will consume.

15. Use your cruise control.

When it is safe to do so, use your cruise control. On long trips where the road is mostly level, use your cruise control. Cruise control will take away random bursts of speed by keeping the car moving at a steady pace. Keeping the engine running at a steady pace, as was discussed in tip number fourteen, improves your gas mileage. Cruise control also diminishes the potential for "speed creep," the insidious tendency to slowly increase speed on long trips.

Cruise control is not so great on hilly or mountainous roads because it forces your car to try to maintain a steady speed despite the grade of the hill you are trying to climb.

Cruise control is also not as beneficial if you are a skilled driver. A skilled driver will be paying attention to driving for the best fuel efficiency. This driver will be paying attention to the tachometer and revolutions per minute, miles per gallon economy meter, hills, traffic patterns, and many other things—not just speed. Remember the egg underfoot.

Bonus tip: If your car does not have cruise control, safely follow another driver who has cruise control or who looks like they are driving fuel efficiently.

16. Remove the junk from your trunk.

What is in your trunk? Is your car a storage unit on wheels? If so, then you're burning gas needlessly. Heavy objects reduce fuel efficiency by increasing the burden on your engine by means of extra overall car weight.

According to the Federal Trade Commission (FTC), our nation's consumer protection agency, adding one hundred pounds to our car will reduce fuel efficiency by up to 2 percent ("Good, Better, Best: How to Improve gas Mileage"). So, remove the junk from your trunk!

Bonus tip: Other than just removing junk, how about removing extra seats? If you have a large vehicle that has a third row of seats, remove them when they are not needed. An idea for truck owners would be to remove the seldom-used gate extender when you do not need it as well as removing any other unnecessary items being hauled in the truck's bed.

Caution: Do not take this to an extreme by removing your spare tire, necessary tools, or any kind of first aid or safety equipment.

17. When you have to travel heavy, carry and/or pack as much as possible inside your vehicle.

When you're going on a trip and you need all your seating or extra gear, carry your things inside the vehicle versus on top of your vehicle.

The FTC reports that a loaded roof rack creates greater wind resistance, resulting in decreased fuel efficiency by 5 percent (Good, Better, Best: How to Improve Gas Mileage).

Bonus tip: Another idea would be to tow your extra gear behind your car versus stacking things on top. This will decrease wind resistance because the trailer can draft closely behind your vehicle.

18. Don't stop and start multiple times at a stop sign.

I uncovered this tactic one morning while driving to work. I came upon an intersection with a malfunctioning traffic light. It was flashing red, and I was on-again off-again with the accelerator and brake as each car advanced through the intersection. This was frustrating because I quickly realized I was wasting gas. I then realized that I do this at stop signs as well.

Remember, each time you need to overcome inertia (getting your very heavy car rolling from a dead stop) you are using the accelerator, and you are using gas. Each time you use the brake to come to a stop you are losing the momentum that was gained from acceleration (you're wasting the gas used to get you rolling). This is similar to the discussion in tip fourteen.

The traffic patterns at stop signs and stoplights change constantly. Each time you come to a stop sign you will be using a different amount of gas depending on the number of cars in front of you. You should attempt to keep a safe distance and try not to come to a complete stop, except when it is your turn at the front of the line (I'm sure you and all your police friends will appreciate that little piece of advice).

19. Close your windows and sunroof.

When you are traveling at highway speeds and your window(s) and/or sunroof is open, you are creating drag. This reduces your gas mileage. The drag is created as the air you are passing through gets sucked into the car without having the ability to exit the car at the same rate it entered. This acts like a brake on the car.

Bonus tip: If you do have a sunroof, purchase an aerodynamic sunroof visor that prevents to much air from being sucked into the cabin.

20. Remove the unused rack.

The roof rack, ski rack, luggage rack, or bike rack that is not being used is using up gas. These unused racks add weight to your car; they are also creating aerodynamic drag.

Bonus tip: The permanent rack on your SUV, wagon, or minivan creates drag all the time. You can decrease this drag by removing the rack's crossbars.

21. Use your air conditioning wisely.

Air conditioning is a wonderful thing, and I imagine most people cannot do without it. I am one of these people. In the four cars I tested, I could not unequivocally prove that using the air conditioner significantly reduced the car's fuel efficiency, but if you think about the mechanical drag placed on the engine by having you're AC on, it makes sense that your fuel mileage will be reduced a little. However, the bottom line is for you to be comfortable.

The Environmental Protection Agency (EPA) will soon shed some light on this topic. In 2008, the EPA will change its fuel efficiency tests to include cars driven while using the AC. In addition to adding AC factors into the fuel-efficiency equation, the EPA will also test cars at an increased highway speed, and the EPA will conduct a rapid acceleration test.

According to an article in the December 2006 Consumer Reports magazine, "The U.S. Environmental Protection Agency has established a new method for determining miles-per-gallon estimates that appear on vehicle window stickers. This change will take effect on all 2008 models and is expected to show a significant decrease in city and highway fuel-economy estimates that better reflect real-world driving. They are expected to drop 12% on average for city miles per gallon, but it could be as much as 30%, depending on the model. The highway miles per gallon estimates are expected to fall an average of 8%, but could reach 25% on some vehicles" ("EPA Establishes More Real-World Fuel-Economy Tests").

Bonus tip: Try driving with the windows open on days that are not that hot, but remember, driving fast with the windows open creates drag and reduces miles per gallon. Lower the windows at speeds under 40 mph.

Bonus tip: Before you use your AC, ventilate the cabin by opening the windows and turning on the fan to remove the hot air in the ventilation system. This will help you and your car cool down quicker.

Bonus tip: Use the recirculate control mode when using your AC. Recirculating air that is already cool allows the AC system to do less work.

Bonus tip: Turn off your AC before you park. It will still be cool in your cabin during the final few minutes of your journey.

22. Using the fan is no better than running the air conditioner.

This might seem like a good option, but the fan like the air conditioner increases the load or mechanical drag on the engine. This increased load decreases your miles per gallon a little.

23. Look and plan ahead when approaching hills or small rises in the road.

Look down the road and plan for the hill ahead of you. If you want to save gas without losing too much of your momentum, safely accelerate *before* you are on the hill. Accelerating while going uphill greatly increases your fuel consumption due to two main reasons. First, any acceleration at all consumes a lot of fuel, and second, you are pushing a two- to three-ton vehicle uphill.

Bonus tip: Avoid taking routes that have a lot of hills. This also applies to small and or gradual inclines in the road. Having a heavy right foot going uphill will cost you dearly at the pump. Many times it is possible to do more of the needed acceleration to get over the hill before the hill actually starts.

24. Look and plan ahead when going downhill.

Just the opposite of going uphill, plan your descent of a small hill or a gentle slope by coasting as long as possible. The longer you are safely off or are pressing lightly on the accelerator, the better gas mileage you will get. Safely use the slope of the hill and gravity to your benefit.

The following are some things to consider. If you are solely relying on your brakes to control your descent, they may overheat and fail. On long hills or steep downgrades, do not turn off your engine to save gas because you may lose power to your steering or your brakes and you may accidentally remove your key from the steering column. This could in turn lock up the steering column. Do not disengage your transmission; this will decrease the control you have over your vehicle and this may cause damage to your transmission.

25. Don't tailgate.

If you are following the driver ahead of you too closely, you will more than likely need to hit your brakes hard and frequently when that driver slows down. This is ultimately expensive to the tailgater because in city driving, and even on the highway, you are forced to be on-again off-again on both the brake and the accelerator with great frequency.

Tailgating is also unwise and unsafe because of the unpredictable nature of traffic and other drivers. The increased unpredictability reduces your ability to best control your miles per gallon, and more importantly, your car.

A good rule of thumb is to remain three seconds behind the vehicle ahead of you. The faster you drive, the more time and space you will need. Also, remember to allow for more time and space during bad weather conditions.

26. Let 'em roll.

Coast, cruise, and let 'em roll. This tip is similar to tip number twenty-four, but it is focused more on traffic-pattern awareness than on gravity. Look down the road to see if you can let off the gas and coast up to a stoplight or stop sign. Once again, the less time your right foot spends on the accelerator, the greater miles per gallon you will achieve.

Bonus tip: Pay attention to traffic patterns and create a safe driving space for yourself. Be aware of the traffic and driving conditions around you at all times by being an alert, safe, and defensive driver. The following are some of the things you need to pay attention to: other drivers, road conditions, weather conditions, the density of traffic, and the speed or flow of traffic. Be conscientious of the size and type of road or highway you are using. Ask yourself how knowledgeable and familiar you are with the road you are using, and know the directions you need to take.

27. Don't wait to pass another driver.

As soon as you can see you will be passing a slower driver, do it, but please do it safely. Don't wait to pass and get stuck behind a slower vehicle. This will reduce your momentum, and then you will need to accelerate to get back up to a safe passing speed, which could force you to increase your speed above what you were cruising at previously. All this activity wastes gas.

Please keep in mind the traffic and driving conditions mentioned above in tip number twenty-six.

28. Turn corners in a fuel-efficient manner.

When it's time to navigate a corner, most of us hit the brakes pretty hard to slow down prior to making the turn. Then, once we have turned the corner, we accelerate hard out of the turn. This method wastes a lot of gas.

A more fuel-efficient way to navigate turns is to plan the turn using as little mechanical braking as possible. Plan to decrease your speed by lifting off the accelerator, coasting to a safe turning speed instead of hitting the brakes (just remember always to be safe), and then smoothly and gently accelerate out of the turn.

When you hit the brake to turn the corner, you are wasting valuable momentum and gas that you gained from acceleration. Also, remember to accelerate out of a turn gently; don't hit the accelerator hard (it's that egg under your foot again). These ideas will gain you valuable miles per gallon while putting less wear and tear on your braking system, your engine, your tires, and many other parts of your vehicle. Try to smooth out your braking and your acceleration around corners. It is not a race!

29. Time the traffic lights.

DON'T FORGET

Have you ever noticed that when you're in a hurry, it seems as if you get held up all the lights? Traffic lights are often timed to keep the traffic flowing for people who are driving at the speed limit. Based on that theory, one can assume that traveling at a steady, legal pace (the speed limit) will increase your chances of cruising through the lights instead of being caught at them.

Bonus tip: Don't negotiate traffic lights and intersections hastily or unsafely. This tip assumes you are looking a fair distance down the road. When you see a green light in front of you, there is a good chance it will be turning red soon, so prepare for this by lifting your foot off the gas pedal. Not only is this safe, it also saves you gas. To some degree, you can also use this tip if the light in front of you is presently red, again assuming you are looking a fair distance down the road. You can guess that it may change by the time you get there. Just be safe.

Bonus tip: This tip is minor, but as I've said before, it's the cumulative effect that counts. Time your entry into your garage by opening the garage door with your garage door opener. You can also do this at electronically controlled fences or gates. In both examples, you use your existing momentum versus stopping and starting which wastes gas.

30. What's your left foot doing?

Don't allow your left foot to rest on the brake or clutch while driving. The slightest pressure on the brake puts a mechanical drag on the engine.

If you're depressing the clutch with your left foot, you are releasing the contact pressure in the transmission. This decreases fuel efficiency by allowing slippage in the drive train (engine and transmission) mechanisms. This slight pressure on either the brake or clutch also creates a great deal of unnecessary wear and tear on these very expensive components.

31. What kind of music are you listening to?

I know this one sounds crazy, but think about it for a minute. If you are cruising along listening to soft rock, cool jazz, or classical music (or any other calming music), I bet your driving habits are more controlled than if you were driving to some really fast-paced hard rock, rap, or heavy metal.

Also, think of the emotional impact the song lyrics may have on you. This is a psychological and an emotional tip for saving gas. If you are listening to a song that gets you pumped up, excites you, or makes you anxious, your driving style changes.

32. Keep it in drive.

Try to park where you can pull away from your parking spot in *drive* versus having to reverse out and then put the car into drive. Reverse is not a fuel-efficient gear, and each time you engage the reverse gear, you step on the accelerator and then stop, only to once again put the car in drive and step on the accelerator a second time to move forward. This is not a very fuel-efficient process.

33. Carpool, rideshare, take a bus, telecommute, or work a flexible schedule.

Here we have many tips rolled into one.

Share the burden of the pump. Take turns driving with a friend or two when you're commuting. This practice will also increase the longevity of your car, because you are using it less. In addition to the gas savings, if you live in an area of the country that has toll roads, you can also share these precious dollars.

If your company sponsors or supports a rideshare program, try to use it. With gas prices going nowhere but up, now is the time to take a serious new look at this option.

Take the bus or other public transport. Are you living in a place where public transportation is available? Can you walk, ride a bike, or share a ride with a friend? These are all options that are available to us. We underestimate our capabilities when it comes to getting around without our cars. Our dependence on cars can be decreased. Using public transportation is another way to achieve this.

Another idea would be to telecommute as often as you can if your job permits this. This could save you one complete round-trip to work each week, and take your car off the road one day a week for everyone else.

Another idea would be to ask your employer if you can work four, ten-hour days instead of five, eight-hour days. Some companies call this a flexible schedule while others call these hours flexi-hours.

34. Change the car you drive.

This is one of the easiest and most obvious ways you can save gas. Trading the car you drive on a daily basis to a far more fuel-efficient car has the potential to save you hundreds and maybe thousands of dollars each year. Depending on what you are presently driving, it may also prove to be less expensive. Your monthly payments could be less than you are already paying and your auto insurance could decrease. As an additional bonus, many new cars come with no maintenance contracts, which means that repairs and maintenance are free for a set time or mileage.

Based on the simple observation of one person driving a vehicle built to carry five to eight occupants, many motorists don't really need a big SUV or pickup. Trading a vehicle that gets, say, 15 mpg for one that gets 30 mpg represents a 50% increase in fuel economy. By buying a more rational, fuel-efficient vehicle, it's easy for consumers to significantly reduce their fuel bill.

35. Use the vehicle that is best suited for the job.

If you're driving to and from work on your own, you do not need to drive a big car. On the other hand, if you're going to your local hardware store to pick up some lumber, you will need something more than a small compact car. The idea here is that families seldom need two or more big vehicles.

Bonus tip: Reduce the number of cars you have. It is nice to have the convenience of many vehicle choices, but it is possible to have too many choices. And remember, every vehicle you have needs to be maintained, stored, and insured.

36. Put down the cell phone and stop any other multi-tasking activities.

Despite it being a very dangerous thing to drive while multi-tasking, it is also not fuel efficient. By now, you may have realized that one of the best ways to save gas is to be an alert, aware, and steady driver. You cannot concentrate on being fuel efficient and driving safely while eating, talking on the cell phone, doing your makeup, and filling in a crossword or sudoku puzzle. These driving distractions make you an unsafe driver, and they take away from your concentration on being a mileage master.

37. Don't leave your car running.

I would not have thought of adding this one, except that I saw it happen while writing this book. I was in a donut shop and the guy behind me left his car running while he came in to buy his donuts and coffee. Not only is this a waste of gas, it is also a high risk activity because this is a car just asking to be stolen. The car could also become a safety liability if it is hit while running.

38. Drive the straightest line you possibly can.

Frequent lane changes and swerving in and out of traffic increase your miles traveled, and of course, increase your fuel consumption because you are on-again off-again on both the gas pedal and brake. I can also imagine that if you are engaging in this type of unsafe driving, you are also not paying attention to the many fuel-efficient driving habits discussed in this book.

39. Listen to the radio for traffic reports.

Listen for reported accidents and avoid congested roads. Taking an alternative, less-congested route will reduce your fuel consumption, and it may help you get to your destination more relaxed and on schedule. This practice can keep you out of some of the worst stop-and-go traffic there is, traffic jams.

40. Do not draft.

Drafting is like tailgating. Drafting is when you closely follow another vehicle by following in its slipstream. You will see this practice used frequently on the open highway when a car drafts behind a big rig to save fuel. This type of driving is reserved for race car drivers. You are not a race car driver!

Drafting is not a good idea and it is very unsafe. It will save minimal amounts of fuel because of the unpredictability of the driver you are following. When he slows, you slow; when he accelerates, you do too. You're not really benefiting from this dangerous game, and you are not a NASCAR driver. If you are a NASCAR driver, you should know better than to do this on public roads.

41. Park more efficiently.

Since I began this chapter at the point prior to getting into the car, I felt it appropriate to end this chapter by discussing getting out of the car.

When you come to your final stop, place the car in park and engage the parking brake. Then immediately shut off the engine. Do not sit there with the engine running (wasting gas) while organizing your day in your mind or while putting up the sun shade or while listening to the end of one of your favorite songs. You can do all this after the engine is off. This is another fuel-saving tip that seems obvious, but I have seen people do this over and over, and I've even done it a few times myself.

Second Gear:
What You Drive

All of your personal efforts aside, the style, condition, and size of the car you drive determines the amount of money you spend on gas. The difference between a car that gets 20 mpg and a car that gets 40 mpg amounts to $1,125 per year, assuming that gas costs three dollars per gallon and you drive fifteen thousand miles per year. If you run these numbers out five years, the 40-mpg car will save you $5,625 over the 20-mpg car.

Let's run the same numbers again but this time we will use a gasoline price of four dollars per gallon and then five dollars per gallon. At four dollars per gallon you will save $7,500 over five years in a 40-mpg car versus a 20-mpg car, and at five dollars per gallon you will save almost $10,000 over five years. The actual number is $9,375.

42. Don't drive a gas guzzler.

All politics aside, this is the most obvious gas saving tip in the "What You Drive" chapter. The reason I have written this book is because it seems obvious to me, and to most everyone I have talked to, that our gas prices are going nowhere but up, and that these prices are here to stay.

Doesn't it make sense to consider trading in your gas guzzler for a far more fuel-efficient and environmentally friendly car? Do you really need a big SUV, truck, or minivan (which aren't so mini anymore) to run errands in or to drive to work alone? Some vehicles are truly too big for our wallets. Many tips in this book deal with your driving style, and your driving style is something you can control every day. This also holds true for the car you drive every day. Use as small a car as you can for your driving needs.

The bottom line is this, we can, as individuals, even as a nation, significantly reduce our fuel consumption by adopting more gas-friendly driving patterns and by driving more gas-friendly cars. When you are ready to buy a more fuel-efficient vehicle (new or used) check out www.fueleconomy.gov for the gas mileage estimates of cars dating back to 1985.

Bonus tip: If you do happen to need more space on occasion, rent a small trailer. It is expensive to buy a big car, truck, or SUV and use this as your daily automobile with the idea that sometime in the future you might need the extra room. Other than a trailer, another idea would be to rent a truck, van, or SUV on occasions when you need the extra space.

Bonus tip: Truck drivers can reduce the turbulence in their truck beds by purchasing a bed cover. The turbulence created inside the bed exerts resistance on the aerodynamics of your vehicle and reduces your fuel efficiency.

Dropping your tailgate does not help. The air turbulence creates a vortex of air inside the truck bed that, believe it or not, is less detrimental to fuel efficiency than dropping the tailgate.

Bonus tip: When it comes to fuel efficiency, ground clearance is not a good thing. Therefore, buying a lift kit or ground-clearance kit only adds weight and creates a greater amount of air turbulence under the vehicle. This in turn decreases fuel efficiency at highway speeds.

43. Drive a hybrid vehicle.

Hybrid vehicles are quickly becoming popular due to the fuel efficiency of having an electric motor overcome the inertia of starting from a dead stop (no gas is used during initial acceleration). The gas/diesel motor kicks in at a predetermined cruising speed.

The term hybrid most commonly refers to petroleum electric hybrids, also called hybrid electric vehicles (HEV). A hybrid is an automobile that combines two or more types of engines. A typical hybrid is an electric motor with batteries that are charged by a generator that is most often run by a gasoline or diesel-powered engine. This is an example of an HEV. The benefit of an HEV is that the car uses less gas. This gives the owner higher fuel efficiency. HEVs also emit less pollution because they rely on electricity as well as fuel combustion.

Thanks to www.HybridCars.com for the following definitions:

Full hybrid is often used when the vehicle can launch forward at low speeds without consuming any gasoline.

Mild hybrid cars move from a standstill position only if the internal combustion engine is engaged. They also use the electric motor primarily to assist the gas engine when extra power is needed. Both full and mild hybrids require use of the gas engine when reaching higher speeds of about 20 to 25 mph or more, depending on how the car is driven (Hybrid Terms).

This leads us to *parallel* and *series hybrids*. According to www.Hybrid-

Cars.com, "In a *parallel hybrid*, the fuel tank supplies gasoline to the engine, while at the same time, a set of batteries supplies power to an electric motor. Both the electric motor and the gas engine can provide propulsion power. By contrast, in a *series hybrid*, the gasoline engine turns a generator, and the generator can either charge the batteries or power an electric motor that drives the transmission. Thus, the gasoline engine never directly powers the vehicle (Hybrid Terms).

The last section of hybrids to be covered are *plug-in* hybrids. Again, www.HybridCars.com explains, "Just when the American public is finally starting to understand that you don't have to plug hybrid cars in, here comes the plug-in hybrid. With the plug-in hybrid, you still will not be required to plug the car in, but you'll have the option. As a result, drivers will get all the benefits of an electric car, without the biggest drawback: limited range. You'll be able to go all-electric for the 90 percent of your driving which takes place close to home. When the electric charge runs out, a downsized gas engine kicks in and your car drives like a regular hybrid (Hybrid Terms).

Here is a little history on hybrid technology that may surprise you, thanks to www.Wikipedia.org: "In 1898 Ferdinand Porsche designed the Lohner-Porsche carriage, a series-hybrid vehicle that used a one-cylinder gasoline internal combustion engine that spun a generator which powered four wheel-mounted electric motors. The car was presented at the 1900 World Exhibition in Paris." The car could travel at a speed up to 35 mph, and it broke several Austrian speed records. It also won the 1901 Exelberg Rally with Ferdinand Porsche driving ("Petroleum Electric Hybrid Vehicle").

Again according to www.Wikipedia.org, "in 1959 the development of the first transistor-based electric car, the Henney Kilowatt, paved the way for modern hybrid electric cars. The Henney Kilowatt was developed by the National Union Electric Company, Henney Coachworks, Renault, and the Eureka Williams Company."

In the 1960s and 1970s Victor Wouk installed a electric-hybrid drivetrain into a 1972 Buick Skylark for the 1970 Federal Clean Car Incentive Program. Unfortunately, this program was killed in 1976 by the EPA.

"Around 1978, the regenerative-braking hybrid was developed by David Authurs. His car got 75 mpg fuel efficiency and plans for it are still available through the Mother Earth News Web site" ("Petroleum Electric Hybrid Vehicle").

Finally from www.Wikipedia.org, "In 1993 Bill Clinton initiated the Partnership for a New Generation of Vehicles (PNGV) that included Chrysler, Ford, General Motors, USCAR, the Department of Energy, and other governmental agencies. This program was replaced by the hydrogen focused FreedomCAR initiative of George W. Bush in 2001" ("Petroleum Electric Hybrid Vehicle").

Honda Insight and the Toyota Prius became the first mass-produced hybrid vehicles in the 1990s.

44. Drive a car equipped to run on an alternative fuel.

Some alternative fuels cost less than regular gasoline. Be cautious however, because some alternative-fuel vehicles get less miles per gallon than regular gasoline-powered cars. A good example of this would be the lower fuel efficiency of cars and trucks using ethanol. The advantage to ethanol is that it costs less than gasoline. You need to verify if the reduced fuel cost will ultimately be an advantage to you and your driving style.

According to the U.S. Department of Energy, alternative fuels include, but are not limited to, propane (liquefied petroleum gas), compressed natural gas, biodiesel, ethanol, methanol, electricity, hydrogen, fuels (other than alcohol) derived from biological materials, and P-series fuels which are a unique blend of natural gas liquids, ethanol, and biomass-derived cosolvent methyltetrahydrofuran (Epact Alternative Fuels). For more information on alternative fuels visit the U.S. Department of Energy site that covers Energy Efficiency and Renewable Energy by going to www.eere.energy.gov . This site has over three thousand documents in its database, an interactive fuel station mapping system, current listings of available alternative-fuel vehicles, and lots of alternative fuel information and related links.

45. Drive a diesel vehicle.

DON'T FORGET

Most diesel cars and trucks get better gas mileage than an equivalent gas-powered car or truck. Modern diesel technology is also quieter and pollutes less than ever before. Modern diesel fuel is also manufactured differently to reduce the smell and hydrocarbons older diesel fuel produced. According to Diesel Forum Technology, "Diesel is the world's most efficient internal combustion engine—returning 20% to 40% more miles per gallon than comparable gasoline engines ('Fuel Efficiency'). Because of this inherent efficiency, diesel is the predominant power source for many important sectors of the U.S. economy, including freight transport, public transportation, and off-road vehicles used in construction, agriculture, and mining."

An interesting fact from the U.S. Department of Energy is that if diesel vehicles reached a 30 percent market share by 2020, it would reduce U.S. oil consumption by three hundred fifty thousand barrels a day (Mello Nov. 2005).

Bonus tip: If you live in a cold climate, an engine block heater can help. A car with a warm or hot engine is more efficient than a cold engine, and it is easier to start.

46. Drag

HOT TIP   DON'T FORGET   NO LEAD FOOT

A report posted on www.fueleconomy.com states, "at highway speeds, most of the energy needed to move a car down the road goes to pushing air out of its way. On the EPA highway cycle, with an average speed of 48 mph, 54 percent of the energy required to move a car goes to aerodynamic drag because drag increases as your speed increases. More than twice as much energy would be required to overcome drag at 70 mph than at 48 mph.

"Three factors determine a vehicle's drag: its speed, the cross-sectional area it presents to the wind, and its drag coefficient, abbreviated Cd. The drag coefficient is a measure of the overall slipperiness of a vehicles shape" ("Aerodynamics Design").

Drag is the force applied against a car as it drives. From tip number twelve, drag is the amount of air a car pushes up against and out of the way in order for the car to move forward. This tells us that an aerodynamic car saves gas compared to driving a car with the aerodynamic features of a brick.

The more you ride the accelerator, the more drag is created because the car is trying to force more air out of the way as it goes faster. As I said earlier, an aerodynamic car (a race car), has a huge gas advantage over a car that is designed like a brick (a delivery truck and, unfortunately, most SUVs) because the aerodynamic car has less air to move out of its way. Think about the car you are driving. Are you driving a brick, or are you driving a sleek, aerodynamic machine?

In the 1970s, the highway speed limits were reduced to 55 mph. This speed limit was enforced for many reasons, but one of the main reasons was to improve the nation's fuel efficiency. If you drive above 55 mph, your fuel economy will get worse; this has a lot to do with the aerodynamics of the car you are driving. Other elements that negatively effect aerodynamics are vinyl tops, rag tops, sunroofs, dirt, luggage racks, bike racks, off-road lights, ride height, the air space underneath you car, wheel and tire size, and many other items that detract from the cars smooth aerodynamic lines. These features create drag by reducing efficient air flow over your car.

47. What kind of tires are you using?

Radial tires are most common today, and they are known for better fuel efficiency than non-radial tires. Check also for tires that are designed for a higher tire pressure. Higher tire pressures reduce the rolling resistance and will improve your mileage.

Other things to consider are the weight of your wheels and the height and width of your tires.

On the station wagon test car mentioned in the test results chapter, I discovered the effect of new wheels and tires the hard way. After my initial testing, I decided to buy some larger, wider, and ultimately, heavier wheels. I also needed to buy new tires to fit these wheels. They looked absolutely great, and the car handled better. I even painted the brake calipers red for extra flare. The downside is that I reduced my gas mileage by approximately 5 percent. There was a reason for the mileage drop: increased weight, increased tire surface area on the ground which increases rolling resistance, and an increase in aerodynamic drag as the wider tire created a greater surface area compared to the original, thinner tire.

Bonus tip: I know this may seem obvious, but when winter ends you should change from snow tires back to regular tires. Wait until it's safe and the good weather begins.

Bonus tip: If you're driving a truck or an SUV, are you driving around on deep tread wide balloon tires? If you are, you're getting worse gas mileage than you probably need to or want to.

48. Don't use gas saving devices.

In a nutshell, don't waste your money. According to an FTC consumer alert, "Be skeptical of claims for devices that will boost your mileage by an extra 6 miles per gallon, improve your fuel economy up to 26 percent, or the like (Good, Better, Best: How to Improve Gas Mileage). For more information and a full list of tested products, check www.epa.gov/otaq/consumer.htm". "The U.S. Environmental Protection Agency (EPA) has tested over 100 supposed gas-saving devices—including mixture enhancers and fuel line magnets—and found that very few provide any fuel economy benefits. The devices that work provide only marginal improvements. In fact, some gas-saving products even may damage a car's engine or cause substantial increases exhaust emissions" (Dubious Gas Saving Gadgets Can Drive You to Distraction).

Think of it logically. If these gadgets really worked, don't you think the automobile manufacturers would be all over them and using them in all of their models? Of course, they would.

49. Manual transmissions versus automatic transmissions.

DON'T FORGET

Our modern automatic transmissions are far more fuel efficient than the automatic transmissions of yesteryear. They are becoming more of a match for a skilled driver operating a manual transmission.

A manual transmission can be shifted to the highest gear sooner than an automatic transmission. This can result in improved miles per gallon because the driver is driving longer at lower revolutions per minute.

Today, many automatic transmissions have more forward gears than ever before. They have lower low gears for better acceleration and higher high gears for better cruising speeds and better fuel efficiency. Use the highest gear that is safe, or use your overdrive gears at cruising speeds on the highway. Doing so will decrease your engine speed, reducing both your fuel consumption and engine wear.

When going uphill, an automatic transmission may "hunt" for the appropriate gear. This is annoying. It is also hard on the transmission as well as not being fuel efficient. You can control this hunting by manually choosing the best gear for the road you're on.

Bonus tip: A relatively new automatic transmission is the continuously variable transmission (CVT), which gives the driver an almost limitless number of gears. According to Wikipedia, "The continuously variable transmission (CVT) is a transmission in which the ratio of the rotational speeds of two shafts, as the input shaft and output shaft of a vehicle or other machine, can be varied continuously within a given range, providing an infinite number of possible ratios" ("Continuously Variable Transmission").

CVTs are great for fuel efficiency because this type of transmission effectively has lower low gears during acceleration and higher high gears for highway driving or as www.Wikipedia.org puts it, "this can provide better fuel economy than other transmissions by enabling the engine to run at its most efficient speeds within a narrow range" ("Continuously Variable Transmission").

50. Aerodynamic body kits and other external body add-ons won't help you much.

Are body kits (aftermarket fenders, front air dams, air scoops, side trim kits, large antennas, extra lights, your favorite team flag, etc.), really aerodynamic enough to improve your miles per gallon? I doubt that these add-ons improve your miles per gallon. Many of the body kits look great, but they add a great deal of weight to your car, and because of this, they reduce your miles per gallon. These kits are often designed to create downforce on the car which increases rolling resistance at the wheels. Also, I have seen more ill-fitting kits or loose add-on parts on cars that actually create aerodynamic drag, thus, once again reducing your miles per gallon.

51. Get your windows tinted.

This will reduce your cabin temperature and will decrease the need to have the air conditioning running. Please be a safe and conscientious driver, and please check your local laws before having this done. The degree of tint is monitored and regulated.

Bonus tip: Use a car shade or windshield sun deflector to help cool your car when it is not being driven.

52. Carefully select the model car you drive when going on vacation.

When you rent a car, you almost always have a choice of the car you will use. Choose the model that will best fit your needs, but don't forget to factor fuel economy into your choice.

If you're in the market for a new car, this is also a great opportunity to test drive a potential new make or model.

Bonus tip: Become familiar with all of the controls in your car and their locations. You will likely have buttons, switches, and knobs located on the dash, on the instrument panel, on the steering wheel, on the steering column, on the doors, and on the center column. Not knowing where these controls are and what each of them does can decrease your miles per gallon because your attention is divided. Not only can it decrease your miles per gallon, it can also be dangerous.

An overall impression of what you drive regarding pollution.
As I said at the beginning of this chapter, all of your personal efforts

aside, the style, condition, size of the engine, and size of the car you drive absolutely determines the amount of money you spend on gas. But what about our environment?

The statistics at the beginning of this chapter are very significant, not only in dollars but also in regards to pollution. A car that gets 40 mpg is polluting half as much as a car that is getting 20 mpg. Can you imagine how many tons of pollution would be saved over five years if just one person made a change to a smaller, more fuel-efficient car? There would be tremendous changes in exhaust emissions if more people in your community used more fuel-efficient cars. The numbers would be staggering if we were to expand this to a significant percentage of the U.S. or world population.

We could be saving significant amounts of money, saving volumes of gasoline, saving our breath, saving the air we breathe, and saving our world. If you really think about the above scenario, it really and truly is not that far-fetched. So please, do what you can to help your wallet, and do what you can to help our world.

Third Gear:
Vehicle Maintenance

Whether you are driving a much-cherished classic, a used SUV, or the newest compact economy hybrid, your vehicle's maintenance will impact more than just your fuel costs. According to an article by the Auto Club, "Now More Than Ever, Auto Club Recommends Vehicle Maintenance Tips for Most Gas Mileage," good driving, repair, and maintenance habits can help achieve fuel savings of 5 percent or more based on average miles per gallon over one thousand miles driven ("AAA Advises Motorists to Steer Clear of 'Fuel-Saving' Additives that Promise more than they can Deliver").

If you want to maximize the fuel efficiency of your car, you must maintain your car. This may seem obvious to some, but surprisingly enough, vehicle maintenance is all too often neglected. There are many things that contribute to fuel efficiency. Improving the fuel efficiency can be much easier than you think. Not only will proper maintenance give you better fuel economy, if fully documented it will likely increase the resale value of your car.

In the modern era of one hundred thousand-mile spark plugs and oil changes every fifteen thousand miles, please do not forget that scheduled maintenance and preventive maintenance is key.

I offer you this warning: In order to make their cars appear less expensive to maintain, some vehicle manufacturers have extended their service intervals to the extreme. Some service schedules, except for a few oil changes, eliminate almost all preventive maintenance costs until after the warranty period expires. This is done to reduce the cost-of-ownership. As the cost-of-ownership goes down, the manufacturer and the vehicle receive a higher rating by consumer groups, thus making the car look more appealing to buyers.

Now, let's get real! Do you think for a minute that a spark plug with fifty thousand or one hundred thousand miles on it is functioning at its best? Of course not. Do you really think that transmission fluids and differential fluids last a lifetime? Of course, they don't. Do you really think that motor oil can go fifteen thousand miles and still lubricate like it should? Once again, of course it can't. So what does this mean? It means that proper maintenance is extremely important to preventive maintenance, and preventive maintenance is important to fuel economy and the life of your car.

In the long run, preventive maintenance saves you money, it helps you avoid costly repairs, it improves performance, reduces fuel costs, and improves a car's resale value.

In addition to making your car function better, the following preventive maintenance tips will also help you improve your miles per gallon and pollute less.

53. First and foremost, get your car tuned up regularly.

Again, this may seem obvious, but too many people wait too long between tune ups. Regular and scheduled tune ups that include your ignition and emissions systems are important to the health of your car and to the health of your pocketbook when it comes to fuel efficiency. It is much like the benefits of people having regular health screens or physicals. A healthy body, much like a car, runs better, works better, and lasts longer if it is in shape, and cared for.

An added bonus to having a healthy car will be that you will be polluting less and contributing to cleaner air and a cleaner environment. The FTC reports that, "studies have shown that a poorly tuned engine can increase fuel consumption by as much as 10% to 20% depending on a car's condition" ("'Gas-Saving' Products: Fact or Fuelishness?"). For information about EPA test procedures and test results, visit www.epa.gov/otaq/consumer.htm.

Bonus tip: Another important and easy thing to do is to check the levels of your car's vital fluids (lubricants). It is important to check the following: engine oil, engine coolant, transmission fluid, and power steering fluid. All these fluids reduce friction, and reduced friction saves gas. Please follow the instructions in your owner's manual and always exercise caution when doing anything under the hood of your car.

Bonus tip: Always be aware of and keep track of your travels under the hood. It is so easy to leave a wrench, a socket, or a pair of pliers on the engine. It is also easy to forget to tighten or replace something that can negatively effect your fuel efficiency, or even worse, your safety.

Bonus tip: Sorry to be such a cynic, but did you really get what you paid for? Have you ever wondered if mechanics do what they say they are going to do? If you're skeptical, mark or scratch some of the parts that are scheduled for replacement or repair. This way you can tell if the shop or dealer you go to is being honest. Efficiency is not always in your hands.

54. Check and/or change your air and fuel filters.

Your filters should be checked and replaced regularly. According to an FTC consumer alert, "replacing a clogged air filter can increase your gas mileage by up to 10%" ("Good Better Best: How to Improve gas Mileage").

Here's an analogy. Imagine your vacuum and the job it does. A vacuum works best (has the greatest suction) when its filters are unclogged. As the filter fills with dirt and dust, the suction decreases. This occurs because the air cannot pass through the filter as fast.

The air filter in your car works much the same way. A clogged or dirty air filter impedes the amount of air entering the engine, reducing performance and fuel efficiency. In today's modern, electronically controlled fuel injection systems, air flow is critical for ideal fuel/air mixtures.

Additionally, a dirty filter will eventually allow dust and dirt through to the engine. This greatly increases engine wear. A good rule of thumb is to replace your air filter once a year, more frequently if your car is operated in dusty conditions. A less-restrictive air filter can improve your performance and possibly your miles per gallon. Once again, you're the judge. While you're at it, change your cabin air filter(s).

A clogged fuel filter will reduce the fuel efficiency of your car. Just like your air filter, a clogged fuel filter will decrease your car's computer system's ability to maximize your air/fuel mixture. A clogged fuel filter reduces the smooth and efficient flow of gas into the engine.

Bonus tip: Because there is probably debris of some sort resting at the bottom of your fuel tank, don't drive your fuel level down to the near empty point. Running close to empty increases the chances of clogging the fuel filter.

55. Get your engine oil and oil filter changed regularly.

There's that word again, "regularly." What is regularly? Regularly differs as much for each car as it does for each driver. Some cars are driven hard while others are not. Some cars run on the open roads, and others are stuck in stop-and-go city traffic. Some are driven in the harshest of climates, while others are driven in moderate climates. Some cars are driven daily, and others are driven on weekends, or even less frequently than that. "Regularly" depends on many things; it mostly depends on you.

A good rule of thumb is to change your engine oil every three thousand miles, or when your oil's appearance changes from translucent (you can see through it) to opaque (you cannot see through it). Another good rule of thumb is to check the oil level frequently and keep the oil at a level that measures "full" on the dipstick.

Many articles advertise and discuss the reduced friction benefits of synthetic lubricants and oils over petroleum-based oils. They tout better lubrication, longer-lasting engines, and a longer amount of time between oil changes. This is an area where the decision is best left up to the driver. I suggest you do the research and decide if synthetic oil makes sense for your driving style and your car. I have found that synthetics appear to work better and last longer but they are also more expensive, so to me it's a wash.

In an FTC consumer alert, the U.S. Department of Energy (DOE) and the Environmental Protection Agency report, "your gas mileage can be improved by using the manufacturer's recommended grade of motor oil. Motor oils that read "Energy Conserving" on the performance symbol of the American Petroleum Institute contain friction-reducing additives that can improve fuel economy" ("Good Better Best: How to Improve gas Mileage").

By the way, the numbers on your can of oil represent the oil's viscosity, or thickness. The hyphen between the numbers represents a temperature range, and the "W" that comes after the first number represents the oil viscosity in winter (the "W" stands for winter). The second number is a measure of the oil's thickness when it is hot.

The lower the number, the thinner the oil stays. In layman's terms, 5W-30 oil remains thinner at lower temperatures than a 10W-30 oil (compare the W numbers), and a 10W-40 oil remains thicker in high heat situations compared to a 10W-30 oil (compare the second numbers).

A quick note on oil additives, if you use a high-quality motor oil and change it at the intervals recommended in your owner's manual, you won't need additives.

Oil filters need to be checked and changed on a regular basis. Changing your oil filter is part of any preventive maintenance program and another way to improve performance as well as miles per gallon. A clean oil filter has a greater ability to filter out or catch small metal fragments and other impurities floating in the oil that, if not caught or filtered, do serious damage to the inside of the engine.

I would suggest that you change your oil filter every time you change your oil.

Bonus tip: Keep an eye out for leaks under your car. At home you can lay down some paper or cardboard to help you identify potential problems. Coolant is generally a green or reddish/orange color, oil is black, and transmission fluid is red.

56. Check for fuel leaks.

A leak in the fuel line or fuel tank will, of course, decrease your fuel efficiency. This is much like a leaky faucet in your house. That little drip, drip, drip really adds up.

57. Check that your gas cap fits correctly.

A loose or ill-fitting gas cap will allow more evaporation or even spillage of gas as it sloshes around in your tank. If your gas cap is not seated properly or the rubber O-ring/washer is dried out or split, fuel evaporation will occur. When this happens, your gas literally evaporates from your tank, and the money figuratively evaporates from your wallet.

58. Check and/or change your oxygen sensor.

My what? I didn't know I had one. A dirty or inaccurate oxygen sensor can waste fuel, cause your engine to surge and hesitate, and is the number one cause of emissions test failures. In a Congressional press release the U.S. Department of Energy reports that fixing a faulty oxygen sensor, can improve your gas mileage by as much as 40 percent ("Gas Saving Tips").

A faulty oxygen sensor can reduce your fuel efficiency significantly because the faulty sensor will send out faulty information to the car's computer. The car's computer controls and monitors fuel efficiency and fuel delivery.

59. Keep your fuel injectors clean.

A clogged or plugged fuel injector will significantly reduce the efficiency of your engine. Fuel must be properly atomized by the fuel injector for the most consistent and efficient combustion. One of the most common causes of misfires in today's engines is clogged fuel injectors.

60. Check, and if necessary, adjust your automatic or manual choke.

DON'T FORGET

Having a choke stay on too long makes the air/fuel mixture too rich (too much gas), which wastes gas and pollutes more. Make sure your choke is disengaged after the engine warms up because chokes often get stuck. If you have an automatic choke, it is best to have it checked by a trained mechanic to see if it is functioning as it should.

Bonus tip: In modern engines there are many vacuum hoses that control many functions. Hoses should be checked for correct orientation, wear, cracking, and loose ends. Even a small leak in one hose can increase your gas consumption.

61. Check that your carburetor and throttle body is clean.

DON'T FORGET

If you are driving a car equipped with a carburetor, make sure the carburetor and throttle body is clear and the choke linkage is clean and working properly. The carburetor is usually located on top of the motor. Its job is to mix and supply the engine with the needed explosive mixture of atomized fuel and air.

The throttle body is where the fuel and air mix. It is most often connected to or sits just below the carburetor. Keeping it clean and free from obstruction ensures better delivery of fuel and a more efficient fuel-to-air mixture.

62. Check and/or change your transmission filter and transmission fluid.

You want your transmission working to the best of its ability because a transmission that moves freely and adjusts properly will perform better. You do not want any drag placed upon the internal parts of your transmission, so keep it lubricated correctly.

Bonus tip: If your transmission takes too long to shift into the next gear, the engine will probably be revving too high. This high-revving engine is wasting gas, it causes unnecessary wear and tear on your engine and your transmission, and it creates more pollution.

63. Check and/or change your distributor cap and rotor.

If your car is equipped with a distributor cap and rotor, a worn cap and rotor will reduce your performance. Ultimately, this will reduce your fuel efficiency.

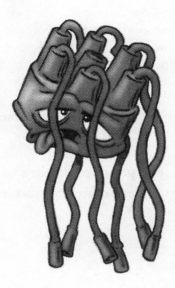

This happens because wear on the end of the rotor tip or on the points inside the distributor cap will reduce the electrical conductivity or strength of spark at the spark plug. The more spark, or the hotter the spark, is a general indication of better performance and better fuel efficiency. So, when you tune up your car, check for a cracked cap, corrosion, and wear to the points inside the cap and on the rotor tip.

64. Check and/or change your spark plugs.

Modern vehicles do not require the biannual spark plug change, or the more frequent ignition point timing of yesteryear. Things have changed.

Today's engine management systems are a miracle of electronic wizardry. Engine management systems greatly reduce the need to change spark plugs because there is far better control of fuel/air mixtures, and the tolerances inside modern day engines are far tighter which means there is less oil burning inside the engine's combustion chamber. This burning oil clogs, or fouls spark plugs. A clogged or fouled spark plug will not provide the maximum spark needed to ignite the fuel in the combustion chamber and this reduces the power and efficiency of the engine.

Please remember, "greatly reduced" does not mean maintenance free.

65. Check and/or change your spark plug wires and connectors (or the equivalent connector boots in coil-on-plug applications).

Believe it or not, spark plug wires lose conductivity over time. This decreased conductivity means decreased fuel efficiency because the spark is reduced inside the combustion chamber. Spark plug wires today are more appropriately protected and shielded from the heat generated by the engine; this makes them last longer.

Another common cause of engine misfire, like the clogged fuel injectors mentioned above, is faulty or old spark plug wires.

66. Check and/or change your differential fluid.

This is an often overlooked fluid. The differential does not hold a lot of fluid; therefore, there is not a lot of room for error should the fluid become overheated, broken down, or even contaminated. Worn or low differential fluids lead to premature wear or damage to bearings and gears. Don't forget, wherever there is oil or fluid in your car, there is a good chance that they are there to reduce resistance. Resistance causes gas guzzling.

67. Lube it, or lose it.

DON'T FORGET

The lube job is another often-overlooked step in regular car maintenance. You may be wondering, "What exactly is a lube job?" I'll tell you. Cars have many moving parts beyond the engine and transmission. Areas that need regular lubing or greasing include but aren't limited to wheel bearings, steering components like tie rod ends, sway bars, and axle grease points. Most of the newer cars are equipped with sealed fittings and steering components, decreasing the need for a lube job. But, lubing helps to reduce resistance and drag in any of the car's moving parts, and as we know by now, resistance and drag are not good things when it comes to your car's performance and fuel efficiency.

68. Check your CV boots for wear and tear.

DON'T FORGET

My what? My car has boots? These small rubber boots or covers keep the grease inside your constant velocity (CV) joint and the moisture out. Most CV boot failure is due to road grime that becomes abrasive and tears into the rubber boot. It is a good idea to have your car's CV boots cleaned and checked each time you have your oil changed.

If moisture, dirt, or road grime enter the CV joint, your joint and your axle can be seriously and expensively damaged. Dirt inside the CV joint will create resistance and subsequently ruin the affected part and reduce your fuel efficiency.

69. Check and/or change your coolant or antifreeze.

DON'T FORGET

Regular maintenance of your car's cooling system keeps your car running at a steady temperature and, therefore, makes it more efficient. With age, your coolant breaks down and loses its ability to transfer heat, fight corrosion, and lubricate metals. A good rule of thumb is to flush your system and change the coolant every year or every other year, depending on driving habits and driving conditions.

It is also a good idea to keep an eye on the condition of your hoses. Cracked, old, or worn hoses have a tendency to break or leak.

Bonus tip: Check that your thermostat is working correctly. This is a step that is often missed when a tune-up is performed. A faulty thermostat can play a part in a faulty signal sent by the computer that controls the fuel-air mixture. An inefficient fuel-air mixture reduces your fuel efficiency. Even worse would be that the thermostat is stuck and therefore not allowing coolant to circulate around the engine to cool it.

Bonus tip: It is also a good idea to check that the cap on your coolant system is sealing properly. A leaky cap can lead to faulty cooling of your engine.

Bonus tip: Also, make sure that air flows freely through the radiator. Check for bugs, leaves, and any other debris that could get stuck in the radiator. The same holds true for the AC condenser which is often mounted on the front of the radiator. A car with a warmed up engine is more efficient than a cold engine but a engine that is running hot is dangerous and inefficient. Efficient cooling leads to efficient fuel economy.

70. Check your braking system for proper function.

The importance of having solid and reliable brakes is obvious when one is discussing safety. Less obvious for fuel-efficient driving is that the brake rotors need to be flat, not warped; the calipers should not freeze or stick in position; and the drums should be properly adjusted. Any of the above scenarios can result in increased resistance and can have a negative effect on your gas mileage and your safety.

Most brakes drag on the wheels a little. This varies from vehicle to vehicle, and it's best if you leave that determination to a professional mechanic. Sticking brake calipers and misadjusted drum brakes are the most frequent problems found in the braking system.

Make sure that your parking brake is operating as it should. This is a good thing to check regularly, but as far as saving gas goes, make sure that the parking brake releases completely. You do not want the brake pads to apply undue pressure against the rotors or drums. This creates friction, which decreases your miles per gallon.

Bonus tip: An often overlooked maintenance procedure is the flushing or bleeding and replacement of the brake fluid. Brake fluid is hydroscopic (it attracts water), and water in the braking system leads to rust, faulty brakes, and brake failure. Failure or problems in the hydraulic system are obviously dangerous, but less obvious is the negative effect on miles per gallon.

71. Pump 'em up: properly inflate your tires.

Monitor and properly inflate your tires. Underinflated tires reduce your gas mileage because a larger surface area connects with the road. This increases rolling resistance, which means that underinflated tires make it harder for the engine to get the car rolling.

The U.S. Department of Energy says, "for every 1 psi [pounds per square inch] you are under the optimal rate, you lose 0.4 percent of your miles per gallon. It estimates the average person can improve mileage by 3.3% by inflating their tires regularly" (Gas-Saving Maintenance Tips).

Properly inflated tires reduce the rolling resistance, increase fuel efficiency, and increase the life of your tires.

Check you tire pressure when the tires are cool, not when they are hot. Checking your tires after only driving a few miles will heat your tires. The heat will increase the pressure inside the tire, and will give you a false tire pressure reading.

As was mentioned at the end of chapter one, do NOT overinflate your tires. This may initially seem like a good way to save gas, but it is not safe as it can increase the chances of a blowout. The practice will also reduce the life of your tires.

On a side note, when was the last time you checked the air in your spare? You should check each month to see if all your tires are properly inflated. Having a tire gauge handy is a great way to monitor your tire pressure, improve your safety, and save money at the pump.

72. Check your wheels and tires for correct balance and roundness.

DON'T FORGET

You should have your wheels and tires checked regularly for balance, warping, cupping and inconsistent wear or other damage. A poorly balanced tire will create vibration in the steering system. You can feel this in the steering wheel when you drive, and the wheel will also vibrate where the tire meets the road. This vibration will create friction, and it will add to the premature wear of your tires.

One last comment: poorly balanced tires and tires that are damaged can be dangerous.

Bonus tip: The tires that are the most round and true should be up front. Any flaw in a tire will be more noticeable if the tire is up front because the driver will feel this vibration in the steering column. The car's engine is generally mounted in the front of the car; therefore, the front of the car weighs more. By having better tires up front, you can reduce the effects of friction and poor rolling resistance.

73. Rotate your tires regularly.

DON'T FORGET

Your tires should be rotated regularly to help ensure even wear. This will help keep you aware of your car's alignment and keep you safer. While your tires are being rotated, also check for proper inflation, roundness, balance, and tread wear.

Bonus tip: While we are discussing tires, take time to ponder whether you have changed the diameter of your wheels and tires. If you have, you may want to have your speedometer and odometer recalibrated. Depending on the size of your tires, you could either be traveling faster or slower than you think you are. Your distance traveled may also be incorrect. All of these will effect your miles per gallon.

74. Line 'em up.

Check your suspension and chassis for correct alignment. Proper alignment of your car is a safety issue as well as a gas-saving factor. If your tires are working in harmony with each other, you will encounter less rolling resistance. Check for front-end alignment (some cars are aligned in the rear as well), and check your shocks, springs, and bushings for proper functioning.

Bonus tip: Another alignment tip involves proper camber. Camber is a measure of the perpendicularity of the wheels and tires to the road. Too great or too small camber will increase rolling resistance and decrease fuel economy.

75. Check lubrication of your throttle linkage (your accelerator/gas pedal linkage).

Most people never check the lubrication of their throttle linkage. If you cannot easily control and gently manipulate your gas pedal, you are most likely losing gas mileage. Your right foot is again key to saving fuel.

The gas pedal should not be hard to depress, and it should not stall or stick in place anywhere along its travel. Again, keep the scenario of the egg under your foot in mind.

76. Have your PCV valve checked and replaced if necessary.

DON'T FORGET

Here's another one of those "My what?" parts that most of us do not even know we have. According to www.Wikipedia.org, a PCV Valve is a, "Positive Crankcase Ventilation valve, or PCV valve, a one-way valve that ensures continual refreshment of the air inside a gasoline internal combustion engine's crankcase."

A malfunctioning or clogged PCV Valve or a dirty breather filter can prohibit your engine from breathing correctly. Wikipedia continues, "As an engine runs, the crankcase (containing the crankshaft and other parts) begins to collect combustion chamber gases which leak past the rings surrounding pistons and sealing them to the cylinder walls. These combustion gases are sometimes referred to as blow by because the combustion pressure blows them by the pistons. These gases contain compounds harmful to an engine, particularly hydrocarbons, which are just unburned fuel, as well as carbon dioxide. It also contains a significant amount of water vapor. If allowed to remain in the crankcase, or become too concentrated, the harmful compounds begin to condense out of the air within the crankcase and form corrosive acids and sludge on the engine's interior surfaces. This can harm the engine as it tends to clog small inner passages, causing overheating, poor lubrication, and high emissions levels. To keep the crankcase air as clean as possible, some sort of ventilation system must be present," (PCV valve).

This will hinder engine performance and reduce fuel efficiency by once again interfering, creating friction or resistance.

77. Your catalytic converter and your exhaust system.

DON'T FORGET

The catalytic converter on your car is a device that aids in reducing air pollution. Keeping this clean and keeping the entire exhaust system free from obstruction will improve your car's performance and your gas mileage.

Installing a less-restrictive catalytic converter and exhaust system may improve the performance and gas mileage of your vehicle. Please check your local and state regulations before doing this.

78. Check your drive belts.

If your drive belts are too tight, they create unnecessary strain and drag on your engine's moving parts. If the belts are worn or too loose, your performance and fuel efficiency will be effected because the various engine systems will not be functioning at full efficiency.

79. Is your "check engine light" on?

This modern convenience includes a warning light on your dash that indicates that your car is in need of service, or the computer on your car has detected a problem. Driving around with this light on may cause you reduced gas mileage. Or worse, you may be driving a car that needs repair or is unsafe.

80. Repair body damage.

That crunched-up front fender, bumper, or hood adds drag, not to mention that your car is potentially unsafe to drive. Another frequently overlooked damaged part of a car is the front air dam or deflector. If your car has one, it will be under the front bumper. Its job is to direct cool air into the engine compartment. These deflectors often get damaged when we park in a parking space that has a concrete stop or a curb.

Bonus tip: While you're under the front bumper looking at your air deflector, make sure that your underbody and wheel well panels are secure and fitting correctly. Damage to these panels can be dangerous. Damage can also render these panels' needed protection and aerodynamic functions useless.

81. Periodically check your car's fuel efficiency.

It is a good idea to calculate your fuel efficiency periodically. A drop in fuel efficiency could be an indication of potential mechanical problems or a reminder for you to reevaluate your driving style and habits.

Bonus tip: Don't forget to have your speedometer and odometer checked for accuracy if you're interested in efficiency.

Bonus preventive maintenance information:
Even though the following may not affect your miles per gallon, it is a good practice to also regularly check and change your brake fluid, your power steering fluid and filter, and all your hoses. This is just good advice for safe motoring and a healthy car.

82. Keep your car clean.

Keeping the outside of your car clean will save you gas. "How?" you may ask. The answer is that the accumulation of dirt adds to the car's weight and surface area. A little dust is not a critical factor, but consider the bigger problem of the extra weight and drag created by snow, ice, or mud. These things cause a significant reduction in fuel efficiency.

Places to look for hidden dirt or ice are inside the wheel wells and under the car.

Fourth Gear:
When You Drive

The way you drive, what you drive, and the way your vehicle functions aren't all that matters. Please also consider *when* you drive your car.

83. Don't drive during rush hour.

Getting caught in traffic does more than just give you a headache; it also increases the wear and tear on your car, and it increases your gas consumption. The start-and-stop driving required during rush hour or other peak traffic times will reduce your gas mileage.

If you find yourself continuously sitting in rush-hour traffic, try to leave earlier or later to avoid the rush. Remember, when you're sitting there with your engine running, your miles per gallon is negative.

Bonus tip: If you simply cannot avoid these drive times, try the following. I have found that if I make a game of this type of traffic, I can entertain myself and save money. I try to keep pace with the changing traffic patterns and the changing traffic speeds by only using my gas pedal to go with the flow, coast, cruise, slow down, and so on. In other words, I try to control the position and speed of my car with only my gas pedal. Please note, this does not mean you should drive unsafely or without regard to your brake pedal's existence; you must always, always drive safely.

The gas-saving benefit of this game is that you only use the fuel necessary to keep up with traffic; you are not wasting fuel in the on-again off-again braking and accelerating process. I enjoy the challenge. It really keeps me alert to the traffic around me, and I am far less aware of wasting time and money just sitting in traffic.

Bonus tip: Road signs are there for safety reasons. They are in place to give drivers a clue about what the road ahead is like. These signs can also give a fuel-efficient driver a clue about what to expect.

Bonus tip: Look farther ahead than just the vehicle immediately in front of you. Use the brake lights of other cars as another measure of traffic flow. Maintaining momentum will improve your miles per gallon and reduce the wear and tear on your car.

Bonus tip: Use the high-occupancy-vehicle (HOV) lane, but please use it legally.

84. Don't drive when you are in a bad mood.

Your mood will have a direct and profound effect on your miles per gallon. When you're relaxed behind the wheel, you're in better control of your emotions, your driving, and your miles per gallon. When you drive while frustrated, agitated, or angry, your driving skills will become as erratic as your behavior.

If you are behind the wheel and feeling pumped up, hyper, or manic, your driving style will, once again, reflect your mood. You drive more aggressively and more dangerously. The infamous "lead foot" designation will haunt you. So relax, calm down, and try to be patient.

Bonus tip: Use your horn only when needed as a safety precaution. Using the horn to send another driver an angry message (no matter how stupid they might be) will make you and other drivers around you uptight. Remember, refrain from being an emotional driver.

Bonus tip: This tip is for the parents of every child that has ever said, "Are we there yet?" or "How much farther do we have to go?" Get an in-car DVD player or use your laptop to entertain the kids when you're taking long trips. Anything that can safely entertain your children will make the drive more enjoyable and less stressful. Ultimately, the drive will be more pleasant for all passengers and more fuel efficient because everyone's mood is better. Please keep in mind that something like this must be out of the view of the driver.

85. Drive like there is a police or highway patrol car nearby.

Have you ever noticed that drivers radically change driving habits and behavior when a police car is nearby? You should pretend that there is always an officer in sight watching your every move. It keeps you on your best behavior.

86. Don't drive during the hottest hours of the day.

Run your errands early in the morning or when it cools down in the evening. This will reduce the number of miles you need to drive with your air conditioner on.

Bonus tip: If your car has been sitting in the sun, roll down your windows before driving. This will reduce the time you need to have your air conditioner running. After a few minutes of natural cooling, turn your fan on to ventilate the hot air in the ducts. Then turn your air conditioning on at a comfortable level. Ultimately, if it is more valuable to you to be comfortable than to save some miles per gallon, be comfortable.

Bonus tip: Park your car in a shady spot to reduce the heat inside the cab of the car, or get a sun shade for your windshield or do both.

87. Take a vacation in the off season.

Take some time for yourself when there is less traffic, fewer crowds, and when gas and hotels are less expensive.

Bonus tip: When you are on vacation, do your best to have accurate directions before you set out in your car.

Bonus tip: Have all your reservations made before you leave the house. This will keep you from stressing, worrying, and driving around in search of a place to stay.

Fifth Gear:
Where You Drive

Your commute has a great deal to do with the gas mileage you get from your car. As has been discussed many times in this book, your fuel economy is influenced by many variables. Some of these variables are predictable, and others are not. The route you take to work each day may not be the most fuel efficient.

88. Stay on the highway versus driving in the city.

I know, I know, I'm an optimist. If the highway is clear, your car can do what it was designed to do: run, not idle or park.

City driving, highway driving, and off-road driving are very different animals. City driving involves many distractions including pedestrians, crosswalks, stop signs, intersections, stop lights, parked cars, speed bumps, and schools, just to name a few. Highway driving should have far fewer distractions and far less stopping and-going.

The quality of the road you drive on also affects your gas mileage. You should therefore avoid driving on unpaved roads. You lose a great deal of traction on dirt or gravel, and this seriously reduces your fuel efficiency. You also run the risk of adding severe wear and tear to your car if you drive off-road because your car was likely not designed for this type of driving.

Bonus tip: It isn't quite off-roading but you can learn to better navigate speed bumps and save fuel by letting off the gas to slow down as you cross speed bumps. By doing this, you stay off the brake and maintain a little more momentum.

Bonus tip: Stay close to the highway when making a necessary pit stop. Also, stay to the right side of the highway so you don't have to travel so far to get back on the highway.

Bonus tip: Is that shortcut really a shortcut? Look at the route you are taking. If it's a shorter route, but it's more congested, you're probably not saving what you had hoped to save: time, money, and gas. Remember, twisting, turning roads may be fun to drive, but these types of roads use up extra gas. If the route is shorter, straighter, has less stops, and has less traffic than other routes, you will save gas.

Bonus tip: A good thing to think about is fuel consumed versus miles traveled.

89. Memorize your routes.

Become very familiar with the routes you travel most often. Memorize the locations of stoplights, stop signs, and common traffic backups. Learn where you need to use the gas pedal more and where you can let off the gas pedal and cruise. Learn where the inclines and declines are in the road and be prepared for them.

Bonus tip: Sorry guys, but this tip is mostly for us. Stop and ask for directions when you're lost.

90. Purchase a toll-road or tollbooth pass.

If your route frequently takes you through a tollbooth, buy an electronic pass so you don't have to stop at the booth and then use gas pedal to get back up to cruising speed. In some states toll roads are less expensive if you use an electronic pass.

Bonus tip: If you opt not to buy an electronic pass, have the exact change ready for your toll. This will decrease the amount of time you need to idle at the booth.

Sixth Gear:
Where and When You Buy
Your Fuel

The information provided in this chapter is seldom discussed but is important to add to your growing knowledge as you make an effort to become a mileage master.

91. Pay attention to gas prices.

The lower the price of the gas you buy, the more gas you get. I know, I know, duh! I've added this tip because we all too often opt for convenience over price. Most of us fill up at a gas station near our homes.

Gas stations situated closest to the highway often charge higher prices than gas stations located farther from the highway. Gas prices also differ quite a bit from city to city. The gas stations nearer to my house are often twenty cents more expensive than the gas stations near where I work. Most people fill up each week, and some more often than that. Saving a nickel, a dime, or a quarter per gallon really adds up.

Driving around looking for the lowest price is probably the worst trip you can make, because you're using gas while searching for gas. Don't just head out in your car in search of cheap gas prices.

Bonus tip: Track gas prices by the day of the week. Prices at all gas stations fluctuate greatly for many reasons. One way to save money is to pay attention to the days of the week the prices go up and avoid buying gas on these days.

I have noticed that in my neighborhood, gas prices go up before weekends when many of us fill up for weekend trips. Keep an eye out for the patterns in your neighborhood, near your workplace, along the highway, or in the areas of town where you frequently buy your gas.

Bonus tip: Use the Internet to search for gas prices. This is no joke. You can actually do this. Here are a couple of Web sites you can check into: www.gaswatch.com and www.gasbuddy.com.

92. Buy your gas during the coolest hours of the day.

I got this tip from an engineering friend of mine. Early mornings or late evenings are the best times of the day to buy gas because gas is densest when it's cool. Gasoline, like most other petroleum products, expands with heat. We are not charged for the density of our fuel; we are charged by the gallon or by its volume. When the gas you buy is less dense (warm), you are getting less gas. Pretty interesting, don't you think? Who knew?

93. Regular or Premium Gasoline?

According to the California Energy Commission Consumer Energy Center, "Virtually nothing is gained by filling up with a premium or more expensive grade of fuel than the vehicle manufacturer has recommended, the experts say. And many of the same experts explain that drivers may not lose much performance from their cars by using a lower grade of fuel than recommended by the car manufacturer" (Regular Versus Premium Gasoline).

You will not get any significant improvement in gas mileage with a higher octane fuel. Higher octane fuels are designed and created for performance, not improved gas mileage.

"The American Petroleum Institute says if you find your car runs fine on a lower grade, there is no sense switching to premium. The Institute recommends following manufacturer's recommendation, but even those manufacturers say it is more of a suggestion than a command" (Regular Versus Premium Gasoline).

Bonus tip: Brand of gas does not really matter. I had a friend who worked in a gasoline distribution center, and he told me that gas trucks from many different oil companies came in and filled up their tanks from the same nozzle. Most gasoline is of the same quality. As you have probably noticed, gas prices change from one company to another. Use the brands that seem to be most beneficial to you and your driving habits.

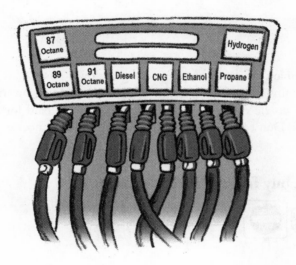

94. Don't top off the tank.

Topping off the tank will very often result in overfilling the tank. This extra fuel will simply spill out of the tank the first few times you turn the corner, accelerate, or come to a stop.

Remember, gas is a liquid. It sloshes around inside the tank, and it can and does slosh out sometimes.

Another problem with topping off occurs at the gas pump itself. The pump delivers the most fuel when it is flowing at a steady rate. When you try to pump gas in short bursts you are not getting a full flow, and you may not be getting all the gas you think you are.

One last comment on this subject: topping off often results in spilling gas down the side of your car. This does serious damage to paint, and the spillage ends up on the ground and in the environment.

95. There is still gas left in the hose and in the nozzle.

When you are finished pumping your gas, slowly raise or lift the hose so the gas drains from the hose into the tank. Depending on its shape and style, the nozzle can also hold some gas. If you've paid for it, get it in your tank. Don't let it evaporate in the hose or in the nozzle.

96. Do not buy fuel additives.

Regardless of advertising, AAA has evaluated many fuel additives, and has yet to discover one that can be proven to provide significant fuel-savings for motorists ("AAA Advises Motorists to Steer Clear of 'Fuel-Saving' Additives that Promise more than they can Deliver").

This article continues, "Fuel-saving gasoline additives are sold at auto supply stores, on the Internet, and through multi-level marketing organizations. Some are liquids, while others come in tablet, capsule, or pellet form; all are added to the gas tank during a fill up." Additive marketers often state that the fuel-saving effects will not become apparent until the product has been used for several tanks of fuel, and all of the companies require ongoing use of their product to maintain the benefits.

Manufacturers of fuel-saving additives also often claim their product has been tested and registered with the Environmental Protection Agency. This is true, "but the procedures they cite are mandated by the

EPA before any fuel additive can legally be sold in the United States. The tests only prove the additive will not harm a vehicle's fuel system or increase the amount of pollution its engine emits; they do not address a product's effect on gas mileage" ("AAA Advises Motorists to Steer Clear of 'Fuel-Saving' Additives that Promise more than they can Deliver").

97. Buy your gas from a busy station.

I also got this tip from my engineer friend. The gas you get from a busy station has a lower chance of being contaminated than gas that sits in a large tank for a long time. A clean fuel system in your car will provide you the best fuel efficiency.

98. Don't pay for full service at the gas station.

If your state permits you to pump your own gas, you can save a great deal of money by using the self-serve pump. How much service are you really getting in the full service island anyway?

99. Go for the car wash discount or other gas station promotions.

Many gas stations in my town offer a discount on gasoline if you wash your car during the same visit. If your car needs to be cleaned anyway, why not get a clean car and a full tank of discounted gas?

100. Do not purchase gas from a station that has just had its tanks refilled.

The refilling process will stir up all the contaminants at the bottom of the huge underground tanks and, in turn, this contaminated fuel will end up in your tank. Contaminated fuel increases the chances of clogging your gas filter and actually making your car less fuel efficient.

101. Pay cash or use credit cards issued by a gas station.

Some stations offer cheaper gas if a person pays with cash, a debit card, or a credit card issued by the gas station. This is because bank credit card companies charge the gas station a convenience fee each time a person buys gas with a bank credit card. In turn, the gas station charges the convenience fee to the consumer. If you don't use a bank credit card to pay for your gas, there is no convenience charge to pay, and it appears that the gas is cheaper.

Keep in mind that you should only use a gas station credit card if you will be paying off the card's entire balance in full each month. Carrying a balance from one month to the next subjects you to high interest rates. At that point, you will feel like you're saving money at the gas station, but in the long run you could actually wind up paying more.

A final important note for the reader
I hope you are willing to use these tips and that you will notice truly significant improvements in your gas mileage. I hope these tips can help you enjoy driving again. I hope you will feel more confident behind the wheel and become a safer driver. I also hope that your efforts save you hundreds or even thousands of dollars. But please remember that consistency is vital to your success.

I found out the hard way that it only takes one rushed day to undo a week's worth of effort. I was late for work one day, and I drove without concern for any of the above tips. At the end of that week, my miles per gallon were far below what I had hoped for and had come to expect. I'd basically ruined a week's worth of effort in one trip. The good thing was that I learned yet another lesson and had more information I could add to this book.

Seventh Gear:
You'll Be Amazed at What you Can Do:
Test Results

As you can see by now, there are many ways to save money on fuel and improve your miles per gallon average. Each of the ideas in this book are viable and very easy to implement. With the tips in this book, you will find many ways you can save money at the pump, and you will soon become the mileage master of your car.

I have done a great deal of research and spent a lot of time testing the ideas in this book. I have spent the past year researching in both an academic and an experimental fashion. I asked questions of mechanics, many of my friends, and colleagues at work. I asked about how they drive, where they drive, when they drive, and what they drive. Everyone was more than eager to help and to vent their frustrations about gas prices. This turned out to be a great exercise. I was able to get immediate feedback, and I was able to get a pulse of the frustrations many of us are presently experiencing.

I decided to see what I could do about making things better. My first thought was to look at what I was driving at the time and to do some much needed maintenance. This was fun for me. I've been doing almost all the maintenance on my cars and trucks for close to thirty years now. I've been a car enthusiast for as long as I can remember. I even owned my own dealership for a little while.

I noticed a 4 percent to 5 percent increase in fuel efficiency without changing my driving style at all. That increase came just from giving the vehicles a tune-up. The vehicles got valve adjustments, new spark plugs, new spark plug wires, oil changes, all new filters, pressure checks on the tires, tire balancing, alignment checks, and on one car the gas pedal and throttle linkages were lubed.

The next place I looked was in the mirror. Over the years I had read many times that the biggest changes in life come when we look at ourselves. I took a look at what I drive, how I drive, when I drive, where I drive, and where I buy gas.

Now I was really onto something. I started to see additional increases in my fuel efficiency in the range of 15 percent to 25 percent. These increases started off small, but the more I grasped the changes in my driving habits, the better my fuel efficiency became. My wife and I have tried all of the ideas in this book and have saved thousands of dollars.

The first test vehicle I drove was my old tugboat. I have a twenty-five-year-old diesel sedan that I have been driving for the past six years. I bought this car because it got better gas mileage than other vehicles of a similar size. Prior to being aware of and changing my driving habits, I was averaging 21.5 mpg in my tugboat. After changing my driving habits and getting my car into better running order I am averaging 28.3 mpg. This is a positive change of 6.8 mpg or 31.62 percent.

The tank in this car holds approximately twenty gallons of gasoline. I was able to increase my miles per tank by 83.2 miles. Take this 83.2 miles and divide it by 28.3 mpg. You will see that I get 2.94 more gallons per tank. Now, take this 2.94 gallons and multiply it by $3.64 which was the price of a gallon of diesel when I was testing my driving habits in this car. You will find that I saved $10.70 per tank of gasoline purchased. The chart below projects this savings for a years worth of driving if the cars tank is filled up 1, 1.5 and 2 times per week.

Savings of Gas Per Year

	1 tank perweek or52 tanks	1.5 tanks per week or78 tanks	2 tanks per week or104 tanks
Savings per tank $10.70	**$556**	**$834**	**$1,112**

The second vehicle I tested was my wife's six-cylinder minivan. I was able to improve the miles per gallon of that vehicle in a similar fashion. I got my average weekly miles per gallon by calculating the mileage driven and dividing it by the number of gallons of gasoline used. Initially, I was averaging only 18.4 mpg, and after changing my driving habits I averaged 24.5 mpg. That is an increase of 6.1 mpg or 33.15 percent. The tank holds twenty gallons of gasoline. When multiplied by 6.1 mpg, you will see that I was able to drive an extra 122 miles per tank of gas. Divide those 122 miles by 24.5 mpg and you'll learn that I was getting 4.98 more gallons of gasoline per tank. Again, take 4.98 gallons times $3.47—the price of regular unleaded gasoline at the time I wrote this book—and you'll see that I was able to save $17.28 per tank. Again, the chart below projects this savings for a years worth of driving if the cars tank is filled up 1, 1.5 and 2 times per week.

Savings of Gas Per Year

	1 tank perweek or52 tanks	1.5 tanks per week or78 tanks	2 tanks per week or104 tanks
Savings per tank $17.28	**$898**	**$1347**	**$1797**

I was extremely encouraged by these two success stories, so I decided I needed more information. I bought a six-year-old, six-cylinder station wagon that I used to conduct more research.

I bought this car because it had a feature my other cars lacked. This car had a computer that gave me a digital readout of my miles per gallon. More importantly, it had another feature that I found to be priceless in getting better gas mileage. On the dash was a needle gauge that gave me constant feedback on how I was doing regarding miles per gallon as I was driving. I loved having immediate access to this information. I could see just how much effect I had each time I depressed the accelerator and each time I let off the accelerator. I could actually see the difference between gentle acceleration and hard or jackrabbit starts. And let me tell you, the difference was huge.

I could see the positive effect I had on miles per gallon by letting off the gas and cruising down hills or up to stoplights and stop signs. I could also see the very negative impact I had on fuel consumption when I accelerated uphill or out of corners. I could see how coasting instead of breaking to slow down for a turn affected my mileage. I could see the effects that a steady freeway speed had on my mileage. It helped me find "the zone" or "the sweet spot" on the highway where I could maintain my desired cruising speed with the least amount of pressure on the gas pedal. Needless to say, I really liked this feature.

According to the car's computer, the previous owner was averaging 18.9 mpg. I was really disappointed by this when I first saw it. By really engaging myself in the gas-saving process, I was now averaging 24.4 mpg in this car, and I still thought there was room for improvement. That is 24.4 average miles per gallon (both city and highway driving). That reflects an increase of 5.5 mpg or an increase of 29.10 percent. Multiply this out by eighteen gallons (the size of the car's fuel tank), and you'll see that I was able to drive ninety-nine more miles per tank than the previous driver.

What exactly does this mean for you, the reader? Well, here are a few ways to look at this in dollars and cents. Take the ninety-nine additional miles and divide them by 24.4 mpg. This illustrates an increase of 4.06 gallons of fuel per tank. Now, multiply 4.06 gallons by $3.67—the price of super unleaded gasoline when I wrote this book. This equals a savings of $14.90 per tank of gasoline. The chart below projects this savings for a years worth of driving if the cars tank is filled up 1, 1.5 and 2 times per week.

Savings of Gas Per Year

	1 tank perweek or52 tanks	1.5 tanks per week or78 tanks	2 tanks per week or104 tanks
Savings per tank $14.90	**$775**	**$1162**	**$1549**

The final car I tested my new driving skills on was a 1987 V8 convertible with an eighteen-gallon tank. I'd had this car for the past four years and only used it sparingly for weekend drives. Prior to being a fuel-efficient driver, I was only averaging 14.22 mpg in this car. After changing my driving habits, I was able to average 19.44 mpg. That's an increase of 5.22 mpg, or 36.71 percent. It's also an increase of one hundred miles per tank.

So, as we did above, let's do the math. Take the additional one hundred miles per tank and divide it by 19.44 mpg. This comes to 5.14 additional gallons of gas per tank. Now, multiply 5.14 by $3.69—the price of super unleaded when I wrote this book—and you'll see that I saved $18.96 per tank. One last time, the chart below projects this savings for a years worth of driving if the cars tank is filled up 1, 1.5 and 2 times per week.

Savings of Gas Per Year

	1 tank perweek or52 tanks	1.5 tanks per week or78 tanks	2 tanks per week or104 tanks
Savings per tank $18.96	**$986**	**$1450**	**$1972**

My test results are based on four very different cars that were tested in real-world driving conditions. I drove each of these cars exclusively for one month. I live in Southern California where traffic congestion varies greatly, depending on the time of day you drive. The area I live in has a few rolling hills here and there as well.

While conducting this research, one of the main freeways I use was under construction. Because of this, I was able to test if driving 55 mph would decrease fuel consumption. The answer is that it does decrease fuel consumption. I was fortunate because I was able to test this fuel-saving idea without impeding traffic or being an unsafe driver.

The numbers above came as quite a pleasant surprise to me. I was really pleased with my achievements, and I found the experiments fun to do. Most importantly, my achievements helped me describe the gas-saving tips presented in this book in an easy-to-follow manner.

If you carefully apply yourself to these ideas, they will save you money at the pump every time, no matter the price of gas, no matter the car you drive.

I enjoyed the process of saving money at the pump, and I enjoyed the process of researching and writing this book. I learned a great deal about my driving habits, about cars, and about future technology that's headed our way.

I learned that anything that impedes the movement of a car, like rolling resistance from a poorly inflated tire, wind resistance from increasing speeds and poor aerodynamics, wheel alignment, and any drag placed upon the car by the brakes or even roof racks, bike racks, open windows and open sunroofs affect the fuel mileage.

I learned so much that I ultimately thought it would be a great idea to pass this information along. A project like this is always more fun when the results are positive and the information uncovered can easily be used by others.

Of course, a disclaimer is in order. Because your present driving habits may be better or worse than mine, because the car you presently drive may be more or less fuel efficient than mine, and because you will be either more or less devoted to implementing the changes to your driving habits, your mileage will likely vary from the previous examples.

Eighth Gear:
Summary

This chapter is written as an overview and can serve as a reminder of the key gas-saving tips for both city and highway driving. It can be used as a quick reference page.

City Driving Summary

Driving in the city requires the implementation of gas-saving techniques:

- Drive smoothly (remember the egg under the accelerator);
- Maintain momentum (remember the egg under your brake pedal);
- Avoid jackrabbit starts and stops;
- Turn corners in a fuel-efficient manner;

- Plan and/or combine your trip. Plan your route to avoid doubling back, hilly or mountainous roads, twisting turning roads, and congested roads. Most of all, remain aware of traffic patterns, traffic signals and stop signs. The fewer times you stop and start again, the better.

- Remove the junk from your trunk; overcoming inertia is a miles per gallon killer.

Highway Driving Summary

Highway driving also requires the implementation of its own set of gas-saving techniques:

- Maintain a fuel efficient constant cruising speed;

- Find that "sweet spot" or "zone" in your car where you cruise along with the least amount of gas pedal pressure for your desired speed;

- Do not change speeds, gears (the higher the better), or lanes quickly or frequently;

- Keep a safe driving distance between you and the car in front of you so you can slowly decrease your speed with minimal use of your brakes;

- Maintain your momentum by avoiding the on-again off-again between the accelerator and brake pedals;

- Monitor your tachometer or keep a close eye on the miles per gallon or fuel efficiency gauge if you have one.

Summary of Saving Money While Not Driving

There are some tips that can be followed that will save you money even when you're not driving:

- Keep your car in its best running condition. Keep it lubed and tuned;

- Plan your trips, combine your trips, or simply drive less by carpooling, or taking a bus;

- Don't drive. Try walking, ride a bike, or if possible telecommute.

Ninth Gear:
Top Ten Gas-Saving Tips

1. Don't drive a gas guzzler

2. Lighten up lead foot (accelerate and brake smoothly)

3. Reduce your speed (Aerodynamics)

4. Drive a hybrid or other more fuel efficient vehicle

5. Don't drive during rush hour (Avoid stop-and-go traffic and heavily congested roads)

6. Monitor your fuel efficiency gauge

7. Tune-up or maintain your car regularly

8. Carpool, rideshare, take a bus, telecommute, or work a flexible schedule

9. Steady as she goes (Drive at a steady pace)

10. Properly inflate tires

Tenth Gear:
Your Next Car

Below are some energy efficient technologies to consider the next time you buy a car. If you are concerned about the future of our environment and if you are concerned about the future of your pocketbook, the most important question to ask yourself is, "What kind of gas mileage does it get?"

Of course you must also consider a car that fits your other needs. Take a good look around. You might be surprised by the many new models constantly coming to market. I am confident you can find good fuel economy attached to a long list of other desirable features.

Four Cylinders, Six Cylinders, or Eight Cylinders

Generally speaking, the fewer cylinders a car has, the better gas mileage it gets. Have you test driven a four-cylinder car during the past few years? You might be surprised by the power and smoothness of modern four-cylinder engines. The same is true of the newer six-cylinder cars. Another benefit is that a smaller engine usually costs less.

Biodiesel

Biodiesel is a non-petroleum fuel that is produced from renewable sources such as waste oils combined with diesel fuel. It is like ethanol but in a diesel version. I think this is a good idea if you are willing to put in the time and effort it takes to find the waste oil and then filter it before putting it in your car's tank.

Manual Transmission Versus an Automatic Transmission

Automatic transmissions are by far the most common transmission sold today. They are also more expensive than manual transmissions. If you spend time in stop-and-go traffic or city traffic, an automatic transmission could be a good option for you. Additionally, the better you get at using a manual transmission the more chance you have at getting more miles per gallon with it versus an automatic transmission.

Continuously Variable Transmissions (CVT)

A CVT transmission is like having as many gears in your transmission as you need. This gives you smoother acceleration and often a more fuel-efficient highway cruising speed. Each gear will give the driver better fuel economy because each has the potential for lower low gears at start up and taller high gears as you cruise down the road. All this adds up to more miles traveled per gallon of gasoline spent.

Cylinder Deactivation

Cars with this technology save fuel by deactivating cylinders when they are not needed.

Diesel Fuels and Diesel Vehicles

Newer diesel fuels have decreased tailpipe emissions, vibration, and noise, and newer diesel technology has improved performance and fuel efficiency. The only downside to this option is that I have generally found diesel fuel to be more expensive than regular unleaded gasoline. You need to weigh the difference between the increased miles per gallon and the higher price of fuel. I hope the improvements discussed above will increase the demand for diesel engines and that this demand forces future diesel costs down at the pump.

Ethanol

Ethanol is a fuel created by combining petroleum and a fuel additive made from corn, sugar, and/or other renewable sources. These have the potential to help out with fuel economy because the cost of this fuel is less than the cost of regular gasoline. Right now, ethanol is less efficient but its lower cost makes it a viable substitute for regular gasoline.

Direct Fuel Injection

According to www.wikipedia.org, "Gasoline direct injection, or GDi, is a variant of fuel injection employed in modern gas engines. The gas is injected directly into the combustion chamber of each cylinder, as opposed to conventional fuel injection that happens in the intake manifold or cylinder ports of small engines."

Fuel Cell Vehicles

These vehicles will not likely be mass produced for a few more years, but when they do get here, they will revolutionize our ideas about automotive transportation.

According to fueleconomy.gov, "FCVs represent a radical departure from vehicles with conventional internal combustion engines. Like battery-electric vehicles, FCVs are propelled by electric motors. But while battery electric vehicles use electricity from an external source and store it in a battery, FCVs create their own electricity. Fuel cells onboard the vehicle create electricity through a chemical process using hydrogen fuel and oxygen from the air (Fuel Cell Vehicles).

The article continues, "FCVs can be fueled with pure hydrogen gas stored onboard in high-pressure tanks. They also can be fueled with hydrogen-rich fuels; such as methanol, natural gas, or even gasoline; but these fuels must first be converted into hydrogen gas by an onboard device called a 'reformer.' FCVs fueled with pure hydrogen emit no pollutants; only water and heat; while those using hydrogen-rich fuels and a reformer produce only small amounts of air pollutants. In addition, FCVs can be twice as efficient as similarly sized conventional vehicles and may also incorporate other advanced technologies to increase efficiency."

Hybrid Vehicles

A hybrid is a car that basically has two engines. One engine is electric, and the other is most likely gas or diesel powered. The electric motor uses no gasoline and is used to get the car rolling from a dead stop. Using an electric motor to get the car rolling is very fuel efficient because a great deal of gas is used during initial acceleration by a gas motor. Once the car has gained enough momentum, the gas or diesel engine takes over.

As described in chapter two of this book, there are four main types of hybrids, the *series* hybrid, the *parallel* hybrid, the *full* hybrid and the *plug-in* hybrid.

Integrated Starter and Generator Systems

These systems turn the engine off when the vehicle is stopped. This eliminates the waste of fuel while idling.

Motorcycles, Motorized Bicycles, and Mopeds

How would you like a fuel-efficient motorcycle, motorized bicycle, or scooter? Motorized bicycles are often powered by two sources. They are powered by you, the driver, and by a gas or electric motor. Mopeds are most often motorized by a small, gas-powered engine. Some are powered by electricity.

Motorized Skateboards and Scooters

Motorized skateboards and scooters will likely fall short of being embraced by most, but they are good options for short trips, errands, or just for some fun close to home.

Turbochargers and Superchargers

Turbochargers and superchargers increase engine power. This allows engine manufacturers and auto manufacturers to use smaller engines without sacrificing power or performance.

Variable Valve Timing

Cars equipped with variable valve timing improve engine efficiency by optimizing the fuel air mixture into the engine at various engine speeds.

But I'm Still Not Sure What Car is Best For Me

That's okay. Actually, after the discussion above, it comes as no surprise really. Let's approach the process by looking at what, when, where, and why you drive. We'll also take time to consider how often you drive.

First, think about the car you are currently driving. If you can remember, think about why you chose your present car. Now, consider how much your life has changed since you bought that car. Have your wants and needs changed, and will the style, size, and capabilities of your next car be different? Most likely they will.

Let's next consider when you drive. Are you mostly driving early in the morning and late at night when the highways are unclogged, or are you driving during heavily congested, high traffic times of the day?

The next thing to look at is where you spend most of your time driving. Are you driving on flat terrain or on hilly or mountainous roads? Are you driving in the city or on the highway? Are you driving off-road or on nice, paved roads?

Let's now explore why you are driving. Are you driving all by yourself, or are there others in the car with you? How often do you drive alone versus times you drive with one or more passengers? Are you driving to run small errands locally, or are you driving a long distance to get to and from work? Do you need a lot of space for yourself and or your family and all of their gear? Do you need a lot of space for tools and supplies? Will you be hauling a trailer or a boat?

I have asked many questions that only you can answer, but these questions are asked to get you thinking about your *wants* versus your *needs*.

Wants and needs are two very different things. For example; I *want* a car that can go two hundred mph, is fully loaded with all the bells and whistles, and has the ability to carry a family of five off-road in mountainous driving conditions, all the while being extremely fuel efficient. In reality all I *need* is a daily commuter car that is fuel efficient, comfortable, has air conditioning, and has enough space to carry me to and from work. The above wants and needs describe two very different cars.

Here is another example: you drive off-road a lot and *need* four-wheel drive, a lot of ground clearance, room for all of your tools and construction equipment, and room to carry three big guys to a job site. This person *needs* a truck. A small, compact, two seat sports car would not satisfy this person's *needs*. The opposite is also true. Imagine the *needs* of a sports car driver and compare and contrast these *needs* to the above mentioned truck driver.

The point of this chapter is that serious consideration should be given to how you will be using your next car and how frequently you will use it for varying purposes. Take into consideration where and how often you will be driving, the approximate size of the car, the type of vehicle, fuel-efficiency, aerodynamics, carrying capabilities, engine size, passenger space, number of seats, etc., all the while maintaining a clear understanding of the differences between your very specific and personal *wants* and *needs*.

Other helpful hints include planning ahead, considering all alternatives, not limiting yourself to local dealers, bartering, and looking at used cars. If you just have to have a new car and it is in high demand, let the market for the car cool down before you buy.

Eleventh Gear:
Forms and Formulas

There are many calculations that can be used to illustrate your mastery of the pump. Below you will find some of the more easy to use formulas.

Miles Per Gallon by the Tank

Calculating your fuel efficiency by the tank is easy:

- First, you must determine the number of miles you travel between fill-ups. If you have a trip meter in your car, zero out this meter before you start your car and after filling the tank. If you do not have a trip meter, log the number of miles that presently appear on your odometer in a log book or on a piece of paper you can keep in a safe place, and then fill your tank.

Before filling up again, look to your trip meter. The number on the trip meter represents the number of miles you traveled while using your previous tank of gas. If you do not have a trip meter, check the odometer reading and log this number into your book or refer to the piece of paper on which you recorded your original miles. Subtract the second number from the first to learn the number of miles you've driven since you last filled up.

- The next step is to establish the number of gallons of gasoline that were used. In step one, you filled your tank and drove your car until your gas tank needed filling again. When you fill up your tank the second time, make a note of the number of gallons it takes to re-fill your tank. Another place to look is on your receipt.

- Step three is to take the number of miles you have driven and divide this number by the amount of gas you used. Here is an example: I fill my tank and zero out my trip meter; I drive the car for a week and am ready to refill my tank; I refill my tank with twenty gallons of gas and my trip meter shows I drove four hundred twenty miles since my last fill-up. Take the number of miles driven (four hundred twenty) and divide this by the number of gallons it took to refill the tank (twenty). Your miles per gallon is twenty-one.

Percentage Change

To see how much you have improved from a percentage basis, you will need your old average miles per gallon and your new average miles per gallon.

- Take your new and improved average miles per gallon and subtract this from your old average miles per gallon. This will give you the number of miles per gallon improvement today versus how you used to drive. Here is an example: my new miles per gallon is twenty-one and my old miles per gallon is sixteen. I subtract sixteen from twenty-one and get an improvement of 5 mpg.

- Take the number of miles you have improved by and divide it by the old average miles per gallon. Then multiply the result by one hundred. This will give you your percentage change. I hope it's a big number.

Here is the example continued from above: your old average miles per gallon is sixteen and your new average miles per gallon is twenty-one. Take the sixteen and subtract it from twenty-one and we get 5 mpg improvement. Now take this improvement and divide it by your old average miles per gallon. It looks like this: $5 \div 16 = .3125$. Now take 0.3125 and multiply by one hundred. It looks like this: $0.3125 \times 100 = 31.25$. This means that you've accomplished 31.25 percent positive change. Good going!

Mileage Log Form

The mileage log form below is created in its most simple format. You can create your own to include date, specific car, cost per tank of gasoline, percentage change, etc.

Mileage Log Form			
Odometer Reading (at time of fill-up)	**Miles Driven** (current odometer reading minus previous odometer reading)	**Gallons** (pumped or required) Note: miles per gallon estimates are often more accurate if you fill the tank each time	**MilesPer Gallon or Fuel Efficiency** (miles driven divided by the number of gallons pumped)

Twelfth Gear: Conclusions and "Smiles Per Gallon"

I hope you see you are in far more control of your gas burden than you ever realized before. You have learned to reduce your consumption of gas and to maximize your efficiency while commuting to work, driving on vacation, or just running errands around town.

I like the play on words or the idea of, "smiles per gallon." I've found that smiles per gallon can be gained by driving in a fuel-efficient manner. More smiles per gallon can be had if you are willing to change your driving habits. You are very likely to reduce the number of tickets you get; you might notice things around you that you never noticed before; you could be less stressed and more relaxed while driving; you will have fewer and less expensive repair bills; you will be more safe when you drive; and you will be saving money at the pump. I think that all those things add up to some serious smiles per gallon.

Getting the most out of life is something we all strive to achieve. I think that getting the most economy from your driving is part of this quest. Not only that, it just makes sense to have more money in your pocket and a cleaner, healthier environment. This book is not written to see how good a driver you are, it is written as a challenge to see how good of a driver you can become.

Glossary

Accelerator: more commonly known as your gas pedal.

Additives: these are substances or chemicals added to your fuel, coolant, or oil. The most common additives include fuel injector/carburetor cleaners, pump lubricants, corrosion preventers, and oil viscosity extenders.

Air cleaner housing: this is the container that holds your air filter; it is an important part of your air filtration system.

Air filter: this is most commonly a paper or fibrous filtering element located in the air cleaner housing. Its job is to purify the air before it enters your engine. Most air filters are disposable while others are designed to be cleaned and reused.

Alignment: this has to do with the positioning of your wheels. A properly aligned car has improved handling and it reduces tire wear. Most cars need their front wheels aligned while some cars have both their front and back wheels aligned.

Alternative fuel: this is a fuel or energy source that is neither standard gasoline nor diesel fuel; it can be biodiesel, electricity, fuel cells, hydrogen, methanol, natural gas, propane, p-series fuels, etc.

Antifreeze: see *coolant*.

Automatic choke: this device automatically adjusts the amount of air entering the engine. It automatically adjusts the fuel/air mixture.

Automatic transmission: this is a type of transmission that automatically selects gears by means of a hydraulic converter and a system of bands, gears, and a clutch plate.

Atomized: a word used to describe the vaporization of the fuel/air mixture.

Balancing your tires: this is a process that ensures that the weight of your wheels is balanced evenly. A balanced wheel decreases vibration in the steering components. The driver usually experiences the most vibration through the steering wheel.

Bearings: these are anti-friction devices found between moving parts. Bearings require lubrication, most commonly with oil or grease. Bearings are ball or roller type.

Biodiesel: is a cleaner burning diesel fuel made from natural, renewable sources such as vegetable oils.

Boots: these are most commonly insulating devices made of rubber or plastic. There are two main kinds of boots on your car. Spark plug boots are found at the end of spark plug cables to insulate the connections between cable ends at the spark plug and distributor terminals. The other common boot is the constant velocity (CV) boot or ball joint boot. These boots contain the grease/lubricant provided to protect bearings or moveable joints.

Brake caliper: this device houses the pistons that squeeze the brake pad against the brake disc or brake rotor.

Brake drum: these are metal drums generally mounted at the rear axle of some cars and trucks. Brake shoes press against the inner surface of the brake drum to slow the car down or bring it to a stop.

Brake pad: this device is a metal plate that has a high-friction material on it. The brake pad is the device that squeezes or applies pressure to the brake disc or rotor.

Brake pedal: this is a hydraulic lever inside the cab of the car that is depressed to slow or bring a car to a stop.

Brake discs: see *brake rotors*.

Brake rotors: discs or rotors are attached to the axles of your car. When you depress the brake pedal in your car, hydraulic pressure forces a piston in your brake caliper to apply pressure via the brake pad to the disc or rotor. This pressure on the disc or rotor slows the car down or brings it to a stop.

Brake shoe: this device is much like a brake pad in that it is also a metal device with high-friction material attached to it. When pressure is applied to the brake pedal, the brake shoe is hydraulically forced out against the brake drum to slow or stop a car.

Caliper: see *brake caliper.*

Camber: a wheel alignment adjustment that pertains to the inward or outward tilt of a wheel. Proper camber improves handling and extends tire wear.

Carburetor: a device that mixes the air with the fuel in an appropriate quantity or atomization to satisfy the varying needs of the engine.

Carpool lane: a lane reserved for people who are carpooling and most commonly found on a freeway or highway. It is often called the high occupancy vehicle, or HOV, lane.

Catalytic converter: a pollution-control device that acts like an after-burner to re-burn fuel in the tailpipe. It decreases the emissions of your car.

Cetane rating: a method of rating diesel fuel. This rating is achieved by measuring the time between fuel injection and ignition. A similar rating called octane rating is used to measure gasoline for internal combustion engines.

Choke: this device controls the amount or quantity of air that enters the carburetor. It adjusts the fuel/air mixture entering the engine. Chokes enrich the fuel/air mixture when a car is being started when it is cold. A richer fuel/air mixture allows the engine to start and run more easily when it is cold.

Clutch: a clutch in a car with a manual transmission is operated by a clutch pedal inside the cab of the car. The driver will depress the clutch pedal to disengage the engine from the transmission for the purpose of changing gears. When the driver releases the clutch, the engine and transmission reengage and once again spin together. A clutch in an automatic transmission works much the same except the driver does not control when the clutch will engage and disengage.

Clutch pedal: a pedal located on the driver's side of the car inside the cab to the left of the brake pedal. The clutch pedal is used to engage and disengage the transmission from the engine for the purpose of changing gears.

CNG: see *compressed natural gas*.

Coil springs: these are large metal coils that are designed to help absorb the bumps in the road. They are part of the car's suspension.

Compressed natural gas: a very common alternative fuel to regular gasoline. CNG is natural gas compressed into a tank that is used much like gasoline. It is presently less expensive and burns cleaner than regular gasoline.

CV boot or constant velocity boot: this is a rubber or plastic device designed to protect the CV joint by holding in the lubricating oil or grease.

Constant velocity joint or CV joint: a device that is located on the ends of some driveshafts. These joints are designed to transmit torque throughout the drivetrain while allowing full steering and suspension movement.

Continuously variable transmission: this is relatively new type of transmission that, as its name describes, has a continuously variable gear ratio. This type of transmission is not constrained by a set of standard gears. It is a more fuel-efficient design because the gear ratios are not fixed or held to an arbitrary gear ratio with limits. There is no need for clutches, torque converters, or shifting gears.

Coolant: most commonly an ethylene-glycol fluid that increases the boiling point and also lowers the freezing point of the water in your radiator and cooling system. This fluid also prevents rust and corrosion while lubricating the water pump. It is often referred to as antifreeze or radiator fluid.

Cruise control: this device maintains a constant speed that the driver selects.

CV boot: see *constant velocity boot*.

CVT: see *continuously variable transmission*.

Diesel engine: this type of engine does not have spark plugs, it has glow plugs that remain hot.
Diesel fuel is directly injected into the engine's combustion chamber where it is ignited by pressure and the heat from the glow plugs, versus being ignited by the spark from a spark plug.

Diesel fuel: is an oil used as fuel in diesel engines.

Differential gears: a device that allows each of the driving wheels to rotate at different speeds while supplying equal torque to each wheel.

Dipstick: a device that measures the amount of engine oil in the crankcase of the engine.

Disc brakes: this type of braking system has calipers and high-friction brake pads. The driver presses on the brake pedal, forcing hydraulic fluid inside the calipers to force a piston against the brake pad that in turn applies pressure against the brake disc or rotor slowing the car or bringing it to a stop.

Distributor: this is part of the ignition system that distributes electricity to each spark plug in a preset firing order. Most modern cars have a distributor-less ignition where each spark plug has its own coil. The spark commands in each cylinder are controlled by an engine management computer.

Distributor cap: this cap covers the distributor protecting it from dirt and moisture. This cap holds one end of each of the spark plug wires. It also has an opening for the wire coming from the coil that conducts an electrical current to the distributor rotor.

Drafting: when a driver purposely drives very close behind the vehicle in front of him. This is done to reduce the amount of aerodynamic drag on the second car. It is often an energy saving technique used in many forms of racing. It is very dangerous and should only be used in professional race situations, never by people driving in public.

Drag: when discussing the fuel efficiency of cars, trucks and SUVs, this is a term that is a function of the size, shape, and speed the car is traveling. The drag coefficient (abbreviated Cd) of a vehicle will tell you how well it cuts through air. For an automobile, the lower the drag coefficient, the better. A vehicle with a low drag coefficient benefits by being able to go faster, is more fuel efficient, and generates less wind noise. All objects experience drag when moving through air. The faster a vehicle travels, the more energy it needs to overcome drag.

Drive belts: these belts are seen at the front of the engine. They are most commonly v-shaped or they are a serpentine belt. These belts are driven by a crankshaft pulley. The pulley and the belts transmit energy to your accessories such as air conditioning, alternator, compressor, fan, generator, power steering pump, and water pump.

Drivetrain: the route of power from the engine to the wheels. It is made up of the engine, the clutch, the transmission, the driveshaft, the differential gears, the transaxle and or rear axle, and drive wheels.

Driveshaft: this is a metal shaft that transmits power from the transmission to the differential to the transaxle and then to the wheels.

EGR valve: see *exhaust gas recirculation valve.*

Electrical conductivity: this is a measure of a material's ability to conduct an electrical current.

Electric vehicle: this is one of many alternative energy vehicles designed to be more environmentally friendly than a car that runs on gas or diesel.

Emergency brake: this is an auxiliary brake most commonly attached to the rear wheel or transmission. See parking brake.

Energy Information Administration: provides information and data on production, price and consumption data for petroleum, coal, renewable, and alternative fuels.

Engine: it is often referred to as the motor. Engines today come in a wide variety of shapes and sizes. Most are one form or another of an internal combustion engines.

EPA: see *Environmental Protection Agency*.

Environmental Protection Agency: a federal agency whose mission is to protect human health and safeguard the natural environment.

EPA estimates: these are estimates of the fuel consumed in an average city and highway driving by each vehicle. These estimates are based on data provided by the Environmental Protection Agency.

EV: see *electric vehicle*.

Exhaust gas recirculation valve: this device recirculates a portion of the exhaust gas back into the intake manifold to be re-burned. It keeps the combustion chamber cooler which helps reduce emissions.

Exhaust system: this describes the path the exhaust gases from the engine follow before they are released into the atmosphere. This system conducts the exhaust gas from the exhaust manifold through pollution control devices and finally through a muffler to control noise.

Fan: a device used to draw air across the radiator to cool the liquid in the engine's cooling system when the car is standing still. On modern cars, the fan is often electrically driven. On older cars, the fan is operated by a drive belt.

Fan belt: see *drive belt*.

Friction: the rubbing of two moving parts against each other. Friction places force upon moving parts and reduces fuel efficiency. Friction also wears down these moving parts.

Front-end alignment: see *alignment*.

Fuel/Air mixture: as the name implies, this is an atomized mixture of fuel and air that compresses inside the cylinders and is ignited to create an explosion. This explosion produces the power that drives the engine.

Fuel filter: this is a device that removes the impurities from the fuel prior to the fuel going into the fuel injections system or carburetor.

Fuel injection: this is a type of fuel delivery system that uses electronic control to deliver a specific amount of fuel to the combustion chamber of each cylinder

Fuel injector: this device delivers fuel directly into the combustion chamber of the cylinder.

Fuel system: a system that stores, filters, and delivers the fuel to the engine. The fuel system consists of the fuel tank, fuel lines, a fuel pump, fuel filter or filters, fuel injectors or a carburetor.

Gas pedal: see *accelerator*.

Gas pedal linkage: this is a series of mechanisms that connect the gas pedal to the fuel system.

Gasoline Direct Injection: or GDi is a variant of fuel injection employed in modern two-stroke and four stroke petrol engines. The gasoline is injected directly into the combustion chamber of each cylinder, as opposed to conventional multi point fuel injections that happens in the intake valve, or cylinder port injection in two-strokes, and utilize a high pressure single-position injection pump and common fuel line.

Grease: this is thick lubricating oil used to lubricate moving parts located outside the engine.

Hybrid: most commonly this is a car that uses two engines, one small internal combustion engine combined with an electric motor. Hybrids are used to maximize power and fuel economy while reducing exhaust emissions.

Idling: when the engine is running but the car is not moving.

Inertia: is the property of matter that causes it to resist change in motion. Inertia is often described by the first law of motion from the English scientist Sir Isaac Newton: an object at rest tends to remain at rest, and an object in motion tends to continue in motion in a straight line unless acted upon by an outside force. Inertia is the resistance an object has to change.

In-line engine: a style of engine in which the cylinders are oriented in a line or in a single row. This type of engine is often called a straight engine.

Internal combustion engine: an engine that is powered by internally burning fuel.

Knocking: a sound heard when fuel is ignited too early, most commonly due to faulty timing. This is commonly called pre-ignition. Another common cause of knocking is fuel with an octane level that is too low for the engine. It sounds similar to the noise created when you shake a can of spray paint.

Lube job: when the suspension system, drive train, gears, and other moving parts of the car are greased, lubricated, or oiled.

Manual transmission: a transmission system where the driver actively selects the gear the car is driving in. This is commonly called a standard transmission. Gear changes are achieved by use of a foot-controlled clutch and a hand-operated gear shifter.

Miles per gallon (mpg): the number of miles a car travels on one gallon of fuel.

Miles per hour (mph): the distance a car has traveled in one hour. It is a reference to speed.

Moped: a small motorized bicycle similar to a motorcycle.

Octane rating: a method of rating gasoline. The rating measures the ability of the gasoline to resist knocking or pinging in an internal combustion engine. There is a similar rating for diesel engines called a cetane rating.

Odometer: this is a device that measures the number of miles a car has traveled. Also see trip meter.

Oil: the substance that lubricates and cools many moving parts in the engine. Oil also works to minimize rust and corrosion. Oil comes in a wide variety of weights, or viscosities, for the operation of an engine under a wide variety of conditions.

Oil change: a frequent maintenance procedure that's done to keep the oil clean and best able to lubricate and cool the engine. Oil changes are often recommended every three thousand miles or three months.

Oil filter: this is a device that cleans and filters dirt and metal particles from the oil inside the engine.

Overdrive gear: a gear in the transmission that allows the engine to move at lower revolutions per minute while the wheels move faster. This gear is designed for freeway or highway driving.

Parking brake: see *emergency brake.*

PC or PCV valve: this is a part of the positive crankcase ventilation system that reroutes crankcase exhaust gases to the intake manifold and then back to the engine to be re-burned in the combustion chamber. The purpose is to reduce emissions and increase fuel efficiency by re-burning unburned fuel.

Pinging: see *knocking.*

Power brakes: a system of braking that uses a power booster to reduce the effort or foot pressure required on the brake pedal.

Preignition: see *knocking*.

psi: a measurement of pressure. It is an abbreviation for pounds per square inch.

Radiator fluid: see *coolant*.

Ragtop: another way to describe a convertible top on a car.

Rotors: see *brake rotors*.

rpm: this is a measurement used to describe engine revolutions per minute. It is common to use this term related to a measure of speed.

Rush hour: the times during the day when traffic is at its heaviest.

Shock absorber: most commonly referred to as shocks or struts, these devices are made to smooth out the ride of the car and to improve handling on rough roads.

Shoes: see *brake shoes*.

Sludge: this is something you do not want. Sludge consists of the waste products from engine operation that get stuck in the engine oil. Sludge is most commonly made up of blow-by, carbon particles and oxidized oils. Sludge negatively effects the ability of oil to properly lubricate the engine.

Spark plug: this device delivers the electrical spark to the air/fuel mixture in the combustion chamber.

Spark plug wires: these are electrical wires that conduct the electricity from the coil to the tip of the spark plug where the air/fuel mixture ignites upon a spark.

Speed creep: this occurs frequently when a driver is unaware of the speed at which he or she is traveling and gradually increases the speed of the car. This is a common occurrence on long trips.

Springs: devices that are used to smooth out the ride of the car and to help the car stay level in a turn. Springs are part of a car's suspension system. Cars and trucks have many types of springs: air springs, coil springs, leaf springs, or a combination of these.

Steering components: this is also referred to as the steering linkage. It is a system of components that connects the steering wheel to the front wheels.

Struts: see *shock absorber*.

Sunroof: a window in the roof of a car that opens to the outside.

Suspension: a system that cushions the driver and the passengers from the bumps and shocks of a rough road. The suspension system includes coil springs, shock absorbers, steering system components, torsion bars, and stabilizers.

Tachometer: a device that measures the engines revolutions per minute.

Tailgating: when a driver travels too close to the car in front of him.

Throttle: a device that controls the fuel/air mixture that goes into the combustion chamber. This must be kept clean and moving freely to achieve the best performance and fuel efficiency.

Throttle linkage: a descriptive term for the many moving parts of the throttle that connect the gas pedal to the fuel injectors or carburetor. This should be well lubricated so that movement is unrestrained.

Torque: a turning or twisting force that is measured in foot-pounds (lb-ft) or Newton-meters (N m).

Torque converter: a device commonly used in automatic transmissions. It is a hydraulic fluid coupling used to transmit power from one or more engines to the driveshaft. It takes the place of a mechanical clutch.

Transmission: the gears and bands that allows your car to move forward and backward. There are both manual and automatic transmissions.

Transmission filter: this device cleans and filters impurities and metal particles from the oil inside the transmission.

Transmission fluid: an oil that fills the inside the of the transmission case that lubricates and cools the transmission gears and bands.

Transmission housing: a housing for the gears, filter and fluids of the transmission.

Trip meter: an odometer that can be set and reset to zero to register the mileage of a particular trip.

Tune-up: a maintenance process where the air filters, fuel filters, and spark plugs are replaced to improve and or maximize the performance and fuel efficiency of the engine. A tune-up sometimes includes spark plug wire replacement and distributor cap and rotor replacement.

U.S. Department of Energy: a regulatory agency that regulates and ensures energy security.

V-Type engine: describes an engine where the cylinders run in two rows set at an angle to each other. The most common V-type engines are the V-6 and V-8.

Viscosity: is the resistance to flow of a substance, most commonly referring to oil when discussing engines. It is a measure of internal friction. The higher the weight of oil, the greater the viscosity. Oil comes in a wide variety of viscosities because it is used for many purposes and under many operating conditions.

Vinyl top: the style of roof on a car. A vinyl top can be used to describe a convertible top or a solid metal roof covered in vinyl.

Wheel alignment: see *alignment.*

Bibliography

"AAA Advises Motorists to Steer Clear of 'Fuel-Saving' Additives that Promise More than They Can Deliver." AAA NewsRoom, 26 May 2006. http://www.aaanewsroom.net/Main/Default.asp?Page SearchEnginePageSize=&LoosenSearch=&FileSearchEngine PageSize=&ArticleSearchEnginePageSize=&CategoryID= 4&ArticleID=456/.

"Aerodynamics Design." Fueleconomy.gov, 6 Mar. 2007 http://www. fueleconomy.gov/feg/aero.shtml/.

"Continuously Variable Transmission." Wikipedia. 2007. http://en. wikipedia.org/wiki/Continuously_Variable_Transmission/.

"Driving More Efficiently." Fueleconomy.gov. 3 Mar. 2007 http:// fueleconomy.gov/feg/driveHabits.shtml/.

"Dubious Gas Saving Gadgets Can Drive You to Distraction." Fuelfrugal.com. 2006 http://www.fuelfrugal.com/Dubious_Gas_ Saving_Gadgets_Can_Drive_You_to_Distraction.html

Energy Information Administration Basic Petroleum Statistics. Nov. 2006. 28 http://www.eia.doe.gov/neic/quickfacts/quickoil.html/.

"Energy Statistics: Gasoline Prices by Country" Nationmaster.com, Jul. 2007. http://www.nationmaster. com/graph/ene_gas_pri-energy-gasoline-prices.html/

"EPA Establishes More Real-World Fuel-Economy Tests." *Consumer Reports*, Dec. 2006. http://www.consumerreports.org/cro/cars/news/december-2006/epa-establishes-more-real-world-fuel-economy-tests-12-06/ overview/0612.epa-establishes-more-real-world-economy-tests.htm?resultPageIndex=1&resultIndex=1&searchTerm=epa/.

Epact Alternative Fuels. U.S. Department of Energy, 14 Nov. 2006. http://www1.eere.energy.gov/vehiclesandfuels/epact/about/epacts_fuels.html/
.

"Fuel Cell Vehicles." Fueleconomy.gov, 6 Mar. 2007 http://www.fueleconomy.gov/feg/fuelcell.shtml/.

"Fuel Efficiency." Diesel Forum Technology, 2005. http://www.dieselforum.org/policy-insider/fuel-efficiency/.

"Gas-Saving Products: Fact or Fuelishness?" Federal Trade Commission, Sept. 2006. http://www.ftc.gov/bcp/conline/pubs/autos/gasave.shtm/.

"Gas-Saving Maintenance Tips." Edmunds.com. 2006. http://www.edmunds.com/ownership/maintenance/articles/105528/article.html/.

"Gas-Saving Tips." U.S. Department of Energy, 6 Mar. 2007. http://www.house.gov/garymiller/GasSavingTips.html/.

"Gasoline Direct Injection." Wikipedia, 2007 http://en.wikipedia.org/wiki/Gasoline_direct_injection/.

"Good, Better, Best: How to Improve Gas Mileage." Federal Trade Commission, Bureau of Consumer Protection, and Office of Consumer & Business Education. September 2005. http://www.ftc.gov/bcp/conline/pubs/alerts/fuelalrt.shtm/.

Heimbaugh, Jason R., *Driving Barefoot in America,* 1994. http://tafkac.org/legal/driving.barefoot/driving_barefoot.html/.

Hybrid Terms. HybridCars.com. http://www.hybridcars.com/types-systems/hybrid-terms.html/.

"Idling: Myths Versus Reality." Office of Energy Efficiency, 2006. http://oee.nrcan.gc.ca/communities-government/transportation/municipal-communities/articles/idling-myths.cfm?attr=8/.

Mello, Tara Baukus. *Diesel, Dirty No More.* Edmunds.com, 9 Nov. 2005 http://www.edmunds.com/advice/specialreports/articles/93338/article.html/.

"Now More Than Ever, Auto Club Recommends Vehicle Maintenance Tips for Most Gas Mileage." AAA, 1 Mar. 2007. http://www.aaa-calif.com/corpinfo/05-09-07-tips.aspx/.

Reed, Philip, and Mike Hudson. "We Test the Tips: What Really Saves Gas? And How Much?" Edmunds.com, 18 May, 2006. http://www.edmunds.com/ownership/driving/articles/106842/article.html/.

"Regular Versus Premium Gasoline—Regular Gasoline Has as Much Merit as Premium Gasoline." Consumer Energy Center, 2006 http://www.consumerenergycenter.org/transportation/consumer_tips/regular_vs_premium.html/.

"Petroleum Electric Hybrid Vehicle." Wikipedia, 2007. http://en.wikipedia.org/wiki/Hybrid_car/.

"PCV Valve." Wikipedia, 2007 http://en.wikipedia.org/wiki/PCV_valve/.

"Speeding and Your Vehicle's Mileage." Consumer Energy Center, 2006 http://www.consumerenergycenter.org/transportation/consumer_tips_/speeding_and_mpg.html/.

978-0-595-44379-6
0-595-44379-6

Printed in the USA
CPSIA information can be obtained
at www.ICGtesting.com
LVHW041641240823
756188LV00001B/121